Political Function of Religion in Nationalistic Confrontations in Greater Kurdistan

Sabah Mofidi offers a rich analysis of fierce nationalist confrontations in Greater Kurdistan since the 19th century. In doing so, this study makes a highly textured contribution to the history of religious nationalism by demonstrating the shifting ways in which Islam, as well as minority religions, have been variably harnessed to political projects by both secular and religious (non-)state actors, including Turkish, Arab, Perso-Iranian and Kurdish ones.

Dr Markha Valenta, Utrecht University

In the case of the Kurds, the changing relations between religion and national identity are particularly complex and contradictory in nature. Sabah Mofidi's study presents us with a useful historicizing overview, from a political-scientific perspective, of these relations in the four major parts of Kurdistan. Especially valuable is his discussion of the Kurds' confrontations with the successive regimes in Iran, which is partly based on oral information that is not easily available elsewhere.

Dr Michiel Leezenberg, University of Amsterdam

PEACE, CONFLICT AND VIOLENCE SERIES: 2

Political Function of Religion in Nationalistic Confrontations in Greater Kurdistan

By Sabah Mofidi

First Published in 2022 by TRANSNATIONAL PRESS LONDON in the United Kingdom, 13 Stamford Place, Sale, M33 3BT, UK.
www.tplondon.com

Transnational Press London® and the logo and its affiliated brands are registered trademarks.

Requests for permission to reproduce material from this work should be sent to: sales@tplondon.com

Paperback
ISBN: 978-1-80135-108-9
Digital
ISBN: 978-1-80135-109-6

Cover Design: Nihal Yazgan
Cover Photo by Mohammed Abdullah on unplash.com

Transnational Press London Ltd. is a company registered in England and Wales No. 8771684.

POLITICAL FUNCTION OF RELIGION IN NATIONALISTIC CONFRONTATIONS IN GREATER KURDISTAN

Sabah Mofidi

TRANSNATIONAL PRESS LONDON

2022

CONTENTS

ABOUT THE AUTHOR

Dr Sabah Mofidi, from Rojhelat (Eastern Kurdistan), is a Kurdish studies scholar who researches Kurdish Political history, political identity, and the relationship between religion and politics. After earning a master's degree in political science in Iran in 2007, he completed his doctorate in India's same field in 2014. From 2014 to 2019, he was a university lecturer in Rojhelat teaching political structures and fundamental rights, and at the same time, he was a research fellow at the Kurdistan Conflict and Crisis Research Center (KCCRC) in Başûr (Southern Kurdistan) working on religio-political issues of Kurdistan and the Middle East. He continued his studies as a research fellow at the Netherlands Institute for Advanced Study in the Humanities and Social Sciences (NIAS), Amsterdam, from 2019 to 2021, studying the Political Function of Religion in the Middle East, focusing on Greater Kurdistan. Currently, Sabah Mofidi is working on a project on the change in political identity among Kurdish immigrants in western Europe, holding a postdoctoral scholarship funded by the Gerda Henkel Foundation and hosted by the University of Amsterdam. His articles and books have been published in Kurdish, English and Persian.

Acknowledgement

I would like to thank the Netherlands Institute for Advanced Study in the Humanities and Social Sciences (NIAS) for providing an unrivalled atmosphere of support and peace in which to do my research and write this paper. In particular, I would like to thank Professor Martin van Bruinessen for his kind attention and precise feedback during my project on the political function of religion in Kurdistan, and Drs Bahar Baser, Marcos S. Scauso and Elena B. Stavrevska - the editors of the peace, conflict and violence series in Transnational Press – and other unknown reviewers for their comments and suggestions on the manuscript.

INTRODUCTION

The most important division of the intertwinement between religion and politics is the interplay between religion and nationalism. In this regard, more specifically, this paper deals with the ways in which political leaders and politicians in the Middle East use religion to attain their political goals. The case of Greater Kurdistan as a power arena where various nationalist forces and four states – Iran, Turkey, Iraq and Syria – fight for their nationalist causes, is an especially interesting one since religion plays a key role in the conflicts, while at the same time most of the states and involved forces present themselves as secular. Moreover, while most often framed in religious terms, many of the ethnic and nationalistic confrontations in this region have been related to socio-political rights, not religious issues. In this regard, studying the relationship between religion and politics in Kurdistan will allow me to investigate how religion has been used for political reasons in nationalistic confrontations in Kurdistan in the century between the early 1900s and the early 2000s, and the differences between how secular and religious nationalists employ this political function of religion.

Divided between four countries and being a buffer area between the Arabic, Persian, and Turkish-speaking regions, Kurdistan has become a converging region of various nationalisms, while the Kurds claim it is their land, and, as a large stateless nation, should have their own political rights. The contested region is marked by conflicts between Arab, Persian, Turkish and Kurdish nationalists in and around Kurdistan, while the Muslim states reduce the problems of the Middle East to the Arab-Israeli conflict or the Sunni-Shiite divide (Dehzani, 2008,

1

311). Apart from Iran, with its religious and non-democratic government, the other countries overlapping Kurdistan are so-called secular. Nevertheless, the political function of religion has been considered by all nationalistic forces to use against each other; e.g. central governments have used religious sentiments and conflicts to suppress the Kurdish freedom movements, and vice versa, Kurdish nationalists have been using influential religious figures to push their political goals. The political arena of Kurdistan, affected as it is by various nationalistic forces, is therefore an outstanding case to study and explain the political function of religion in nationalistic confrontations.

In previous works (Mofidi, 2021a; Mofidi, 2021b), I have examined the effects of the religio-political confrontations between ancient and Islamic empires in Kurdistan until the early 1900s. In these two articles I have argued that religion had a political function for the empires in their confrontations and shown how this has affected the proto-Kurds, Kurds and Kurdistan. In the first decades of twentieth century, new states and nationalist forces, as successors and heirs of historical empires in the Middle East, emerged. In continuation of the previous papers, the present one attempts to show how the successor states still use religion in order to achieve their political goals in Kurdistan and asks what are the different strategies used by secular and religious nationalists to deploy the political function of religion?

In what follows, this paper first offers a theoretical overview of relevant concepts, secondly an examination of the use of religion in nationalistic confrontations in the four countries overlapping Kurdistan, and finally, by comparing the various usages of religion by Persian, Turkish and Arabic as well as Kurdish nationalists, it concludes with a discussion on the political function of religion for different nationalists as well as its effects on modern politics of the contemporary Middle East.

THEORETICAL AND CONCEPTUAL OVERVIEW

This research examines the relationship between politics and religion in Greater Kurdistan within a conceptual framework based on two theories; the socio-political function of religion and an ethnicity-based nation. On the basis of these theories, it is hypothesized that the Arab, Turkish, Persian and Kurdish ethno-nations have employed the political function of religion to gain their ethno-national aims. There are different aspects to the function based on the extent of the influence of religion in societies and the socio-political conditions. In this regard, due to the high influence of religion in Kurdish and other societies in the Middle East, it has found political importance, especially in nationalism, nation-building and consequently nationalistic confrontations. For this reason, the concepts derived from the above-mentioned theories are helpful in analyzing the studied problem. Therefore, before focusing on the nationalistic confrontations in contemporary Kurdistan, it is necessary to have an overview of religion and its political function, especially in nation-construction and nationalism, and the relevant concepts such as "nation and nationalism" and "Arab, Turkish, Persian/Iranian and Kurdish nationalism."

Religion and its political function

Religion can be described substantively and functionally. In regard to the substantive description, according to Nottingham (1971, 30), religion includes belief systems, action systems like rites and ceremonies, and communal or social interaction systems like group organizations. So, based on the various definitions by sociologists, here, by religion, I mean a system of spiritual beliefs and practices that is concerned with the sacred and interconnects its believers as a single community. This can be as one of the social structures or part of culture depending on the society. It appears as a materialistic presence in religious foundations such as the church, mosque and temple, religious groups and religious movements. The functional description refers to what religion as a social phenomenon or factor does and its contribution to the survival and maintenance and demolition of human societies and groups. According to some neofunctionalists, thus, it has positive/eufunction, negative/dysfunction or even non-function. As well, it has latent function as a belief, and manifest function as an institution (Mofidi, 2015a, 22-24). In this regard, the 'political function' refers to the "entailing practices that satisfy political needs of the political institutions including parties, government, etc." (ibid., 10). Accordingly, what religion does in politics is its political function. It has different negative and positive political functions (ibid., 29-54).

The existence of a political God and "local God of politics" (Weber, 1965) shows the political function of religion in ancient communities. Moreover, religion took part in the motivational aspects of warfare as part of politics. In this regard, as an example, Xenophon's use of religion and religious symbols like Gods to reinforce the Greek army's morale in his speech for the war council to prepare them for their march via Kurdistan, can be mentioned (Xenophon, 1949, 107). The use of religious rituals and prayers as a means of preparing troops mentally for battle and using religious symbols like flags and sacred books continued into the medieval period, especially in both Christian and Islamic worlds, and then partly into the modern age (see: Murphey, 1999, 155-6). Moreover, the uniting function of religion was considerable during the medieval period. In that age the followers of Abrahamic religions emphasized the unity of their religious

4

identity. In Europe, Christianity was a community of all the faithful including rulers (feudal lords) and ruled, it unified the society and bound both classes to each other (See: Balibar, 1994, 163). In the early modern age too, according to Spinoza (2017) using "universal faith", with little difference from a "natural religion", based on a mass practice and a mass theological tradition had a practical function for a society within which both governor and governed had a common interest. He theoretically justified "a collective transformation of religion, from the inside, as a fundamental political task" (ibid., 31). However, through the growth of secularism in society, the linkage between the classes was cut and bourgeois rose against feudal, and then proletariat against bourgeois.

In this regard, even in Marxism, according to Balibar (1994), religion had an exemplary function for its primary theorists so that Engels compared early Christianity with socialism (see also: Marx and Engels, 1967). Engels wanted to resolve the problem of heterogeneity in early Christian forces, which was like a pattern for him, with the homogeneity of the proletariat as the secret of success. Then, finally socialism could be the salvation, what was the imaginary hope for Christians. Moreover, Marx's own argument on religion is considerable, since he regards both negative and positive political functions. Although, he further focuses on the negative function when he mentions religion as "the opiate of the people," and that "the consoling function of religion can also be a cause of religious power relationships" (Borg and Henten, 2010, 11). Immediately before that he mentions religion, according to Raines (2002, 5), as a protest against "real suffering". For Marx it could be like a protest tool in the hands of the exploited. As some religious thinkers mention, in selecting between evil powers and social order, religion does not select pacifism based on 'just war theory (Juergensmeyer, 2010, 49). Nevertheless, history also shows us, when religion itself has been in political power, like in religious regimes, existing social order, or to express it better, maintaining power for rulers has been greatly preferred, as happened in Iran after the 1979 revolution.

However, religion, which is visible in contemporary culture and in the public sphere in most of societies, has yet partly preserved its political function in some societies. This is in fact because of the continuity of its relationship and interconnection with power which are still at different levels. Religion and power are omnipresent in institutionalized and non-institutionalized forms. They are strongly interwoven so that power has even been seen as a central aspect of religion, while it is also the focal point in politics. Thus, power links religion and politics. It makes religion a preeminent instrument in a power struggle, as well as religious convictions a basis for shaping the people's notion of social positions. In this regard, this is how religious leaders govern or used to govern societies such as those in some Middle Eastern and African countries (Borg and Henten, 2010, 1-7). Indeed, public (church/mosque) religion, in the Weberian sense, has been a potent phenomenon because of its influence among people as an important aspect of power. As Apter (1963, 80) says, "Faith is a source of authority." This source is seen more in religion than in other ordinary ideologies. So, since public religion constitutes power, it is important in politics, as well as a political religion based on it, within which religion becomes a totalitarian interference in the socio-political life of the people, is more powerful than a political religion based on modern ideologies, in the Apterian sense, in a mobilization system.

Political function of religion in nation-construction and nationalism

With regard to the nationalistic use of religion, as its most important political function, the relationship between religion, nation and nationalism has been considered by various scholars. Against those like Anderson, Gellner, and Hobsbawm who believe that modern nationalism is an inherently secular phenomenon, the research of other leading scholars such as Weber, Geertz, Kohn and many others shows the religious origin and lineage of secular nationalism, often borrowing nationalist rhetoric and ritual from religion, religious nationalism as a different modern type of nationalism, and religion as one of the important elements of national identities formed along religious cleavages. Thus, religion and religious movements have played an important role in the rise of nation and nationalism in many places around the world (Barker, 2009, 11; Gorski and Turkmen, 2013). Apter (1963) sees the advent of the nation as a religious event. In this regard, Hastings (1999) mentions that religion produced "the dominant character of some state-shaped nations and of some nationalisms" (p. 4). Mentioning the ways in which religion contributes to nationalism and nation-construction (p.185), especially seven ways in which Christianity shaped the formation of a nation[1], he shows the role of religious factors in the affirmation of nationhood. Thus, in his opinion, "a sort of religious injection" produced "a new national identity" (p. 189).

This impact of religion was such that some writers mention religion as "a sixteenth-century word for nationalism" (Breuilly, 1993, 81). Considering the use of religion by both state and state oppositions, John Breuilly indeed traces the roots of nationalism back to religio-political movements of the sixteenth century. Like Hastings, he also considers the relationship between religion and the advent of nationalism. He shows how powers through religion and making a pact with the church occupied other lands

---

[1] They are: "First, sanctifying the starting point; second, the mythologisation and commemoration of great treats to national identity; third, the social role of the clergy; fourth, the production of vernacular literature; fifth, the provision of a biblical model for the nation; sixth, the autocephalous national church; seventh, the discovery of a unique national destiny" (Hastings, 1999, 188).

that in turn led to nationalist sentiments against the dominant power receiving help from the different religious sects. And, how reformed religion was applied against a church state, then religion against secular rulers (see: ibid., 75-81).

The influence of religion continued in different ways in the following centuries. Religion has had an important role in the formation of many national identities in Europe and America despite the separation of church and state. For Peter van der Veer (2010, 107-8), religion, as one of the most significant fields of social practice and also constitutive of the modern nation-state, was nationalized in the nineteenth-century discourses on modernity. As well as having a connection with nation, it had a productive and necessary dialectic with secular nationalism. Some ideas in that century affected the interaction of religion and nationalism in Europe such as "the chosenness of a certain people" in Jewish people and Zionism, "the revival or rebirth of a whole nation, a Christian nation under God" by Christian nationalists, and "the belief in a new messiah, a savior called by God" (Van der Veer and Lehmann, 1999, 6-7). Moreover, in the 20-21st century there have been examples of community and nation-state building with the help of religion in other parts of the world. Zionism in Israel, Arab nationalism in the Middle East and the formation of Pakistan and South Sudan have been affected by religion (see: Aronoff, 1974; Asad, 1999, 178; Mofidi, 2015a). Indeed, "'the religious' and 'the secular,' namely nationalism, are mutually dependent" (Borg and Henten, 2010, 11). Thus, religion, nation and nationalism are interrelated in various ways "in even the most modern of societies," in Omer and Springs' words (2013).

According to Nottingham's three models of society including a society in which religious values predominate, a society in which there is a combination of religious and secular values, and a society in which secular values predominate

(Nottingham, 1971, 32-34), most parts of the Muslim world are among the model two societies. So, because of the influence of religion among the masses, politicians including secularists employ its function for their aims. In these societies, especially in the Middle East, along with the new function, the medieval function of religion, mentioned in the previous section, is still applied by governors to unite and mobilize the different social classes and groups, particularly different ethnicities or nations, in favour of their politics. Using religion, the politicians of dominant ethno-nations often implement their politics, including suppressing and assimilating the dominated ethno-nations, in line with their nation-construction and nationalism. Indeed, their "nationalism owes much to religion" (Hastings 1999, 205),[2] so that apart from the obvious religious cases, it seems that even the most secular ones also approach religious nationalism, which makes a common or hegemonic religion the main basis for the national identity, usually in favour of a dominant ethno-nation.[3]

---

[2] Against the orthodox modernist writers, Hastings (1999) traces back the root of nation/nationhood and nationalism to the medieval and early modern ages, instead of the nineteenth century. Indeed, his work, based on the bible and its translation into other languages, explains the latent function of religion in the construction of a nation. He shows how religion especially in the Christian world and Europe affected the growth of nations, particularly through language and the translation of sacred books by clergies into other languages. Thus, the clergy converted the vernacular language into texts.

[3] According to Barker (2009), in religious nationalism, 'religion must be central to national identity or at least one of the nearly several conterminous features' (p. 13). For him, religious nationalism not only does not refer to any specific relationship between church and the state, but also to any level of religious adherence or participation. Indeed, religious identification is more important than religious adherence (p. 14). According to Friedland, religious nationalists tie religion, nation and state to each other. They often focus on their nation-states. They use the religious faith and sometimes politicized religion to make socio-political solidarity. Here religion becomes the basis of political judgment and identity. For him 'religious nationalism is not about the representation of religious citizens, but about the religious ordering of collective representation.' The ritual spaces and religious ritual practices are used as means for mobilization. Indeed, "religious nationalists make politics into a religious obligation and read religious texts politically" (see: Friedland, 2001; Friedland, 2012). About religious nationalism also see: "Religious Nationalism: Hindus and Muslims in India" by Peter van der Veer (1994), "Nation and Religion: Perspectives on Europe and Asia" by Peter van der Veer and Hartmut Lehmann (1999), "Religious Nationalism: A Reference Handbook" by Atalia Omer and Jason A. Springs (2013), "Hindu Nationalism: A Reader" by Christophe Jaffrelot (2009) and so on.

In this regard it should be noted that although some scholars like Gülay Türkmen (2018) mention the positive social function of religion in conflict resolution, especially the important role of the religious actors since they have a high level of legitimacy and leverage, nevertheless when religion becomes an element for a nationalism or its supporters against other nationalisms and a tool in the hands of nationalists against each other in nationalistic conflicts, it loses its neutral role and unifying function as a common factor for peace between different social groups, especially ethno-nations. Even in cases with the same religion, each one formulates a different interpretation to use in favour of themselves. In the countries overlapping Kurdistan, however, common religion has often been used by both religious and secular nationalists in nationalistic confrontations.

Nation, nationalism and nationalistic confrontation

Religion, as mentioned, has a political function in nation building, nationalism and nationalistic confrontations. By "nationalistic confrontation," I refer to the confrontation between nationalist forces or movements of different nations including their groups, organizations and states that have conflict, especially a political one, and based on their nationalistic stand against each other. Here, usually some nations' nationalist forces believe in superiority over other/s which leads to a hostile or argumentative situation between them. The term "nationalistic" is related to the concept of "nation" and having strong nationalist and patriotic feelings. So, it is necessary to consider the concepts of nation and nationalism.

An extensive definition of 'nation' is here considered to cover both state-possessor and stateless nations. Because of this, I consider those theories which look at the ethnic roots of a nation, although they differentiate between ethnicity and nation. For example, according to Hastings (1999), 'A nation is a far more self-conscious community than an ethnicity which is a group of people with a shared cultural identity and spoken language. It is formed from one or more ethnicities, and normally identified by a literature of its own. It possesses or claims the right to political identity and autonomy as a people, together with the control of specific territory' (p. 3). Nevertheless, merging two or more large ethnicities with political consciousness, which have their own homelands, language and literature, to make a nation, is difficult. Indeed, they are nations within a state, which I will explain further. However, a nation usually has pre-nation state ethnic origins and its foundations or main attributes include a common language, collective name, myth of common ancestry or common origin, common history or historical memory, common culture including religion, and possession of a homeland and population. Accordingly, they have a common sentiment and image of themselves as a large social group different from others. Most of these factors, mentioned by scholars like Smith (1991, 21) and others, are needed to call a social group 'a nation'. By *nation*, thus, I refer to an ethno-nation or ethnicity-based community with a significant population in its geographic territory as homeland, which has self-consciousness as a group with a common political will.

Based on the nation-state theory, each nation should have its own state. Nevertheless, many nations have not been given this equal opportunity; some of them by force or by choosing to remain within a country with other nations. Thus, nations may or may not have a state. Some nations have their own state, a so-called 'nation-state', though it is often an ideal type. It can even be said that sometimes a nation has many states, so-called 'multi-state nations', like Arab people. Apart from possessing a state or multistate, a nation sometimes also has relevant national groups in other multinational states, to which its state or states become external state supporters. Conversely, there are some nations that have no state, so-called 'nations without states' (NWS) or 'stateless nations'. They are located in multinational countries where some try to gain independence or autonomy, and others have autonomy and somehow have accepted the citizenship of a multinational state that they use a medium language in their transnational relations, especially with federal or central government. According to Guibernau (1999), 'nations without states' are "nations which, in spite of having their territories included within the boundaries of one or more states, by and large do not identify with them. Self-determination is sometimes understood as political autonomy, in other cases it stops short of independence and often involves the right to secede" (p. 16). Guibernau's criteria for nations without states combine both Smith's criteria of nation and Gurr's and Harff's criteria of ethno-nationalism. "These are: community (nation), territory, identity, and desire for self-rule. In other words, the NWS refers to a nation that lacks a state and that is politically directed towards creating such a state" (Rafaat, 2018, 32). In this regard, the differentiation between nationality and state citizenship has been also outlined (see: Gottlieb, 1994). As there are nations without states, there are also non-nation states that, like quasi-states, have no internal legitimacy, although they are internationally recognized. For example, Iraq is considered and classified as a quasi-state and non-nation state by scholars such as Cottam and Cottam, O'Leary and Rafaat (Rafaat, 2018, 1-5 & 25-30). According to Rafaat, "the Kurdish-Iraqi conflict lies in the fact that Kurdistan is a nation-without-state and Iraq is a non-nation state, each possessing a nationhood project differing from and opposing the other" (ibid., I).

Thus, the definition of *nation* cannot be tied only to having a state. The partition of some states during contemporary history is an obvious evidence for this claim that a state does not always include a nation. The existence of multinational states and stateless nations on the one hand, and multi-state nations and the unification of some states whose people are of one ethnicity or an ethno-nation on the other, helps us to see the concepts of nations and states separately. A nation is often a foundation to create a state, not vice versa. Nevertheless, as a unit of international relations, in reality interstate relations, the institution of state has more function. States govern the international system, not nations. Indeed, 'nation' is related to 'people' and 'state' is related to "a powerful and authoritative institution" (Van der Veer and Lehmann, 1999, 5). Thus, nations without states are those which are not allowed to have that institution, though they have territory, nationalist parties and possibly local and regional governments. They have nationalist movements, since they have the aspiration of self-rule and self-determination. Indeed, this kind of political ambition differentiates nation from an ethnic group and relevant ethnicity or other group identity with political demands at a low level (Barker, 2009, 9). Accordingly, the Kurdish nation is a stateless nation and others like Persian/Iranian, Turkish and Arab nations are state-possessor nations. So, the Kurdish nationalists are in 'opposition to the existing states' and the others have 'state-led nationalism', in Breuilly's words (1993, 2).

Nationalism is the ideology of a socio-political movement seeking the political rights of a nation or exercising political power to preserve the interests of a nation-state or a dominant nation in a multinational state, and justifying its action with nationalist arguments based on the above-mentioned definition of nation and its interests and values. It shows "the sentiment of belonging to a community whose members identify with a set of symbols, beliefs and ways of life, and have the will to decide upon their common political identity" (Guibernau, 1999, 14). In nationalism there is the belief that "one's own ethnic or national tradition is especially valuable and needs to be defended at almost any cost through creation or extension of its own nation-state" (Hastings, 1999, 4). The purpose and legitimacy of nationalists are derived from the collective subject they claim to represent (Friedland, 2012), as well as the ultimate level of will in their nationalism, which is political equality between all nations, that is, having a state. In fact, an ethno-national movement or state-led ethno-nationalism is legitimate as long as it tries to be equal or to maintain its equality with other ethno-nations. Going beyond this reasonable level of demands is not nationalistic and leads to chauvinism.

Some stateless nations have nationalism to seek political equality with others not only within the relevant states but also with nations who have their own independent state, while others have nationism since they feel equal not only culturally but also politically with other ethno-nations within a state, like some ethno-nations in India. Nevertheless, even if the political demand of subordinated nations is realized by confederation, federation or autonomy, the demand for making an independent state will potentially remain. Therefore, it is one of the necessities of democracy that a peaceful and legal way of separation be considered in democratic countries. According to Friedland (2012), "nationalisms may counter existing states, seeking some form of recognition within the state, or to break away from the state and form their own. A nation is always a potentially sovereign subject. Sovereignty is immanent in nationhood; nations without sovereignty are states-in-waiting, even if that wait may be forever." He mentions the Kurds as one of these nations. In relation to this, the present research considers the conflict and confrontation between stateless nationalists that seek the rights of a nation without a state, the Kurds, and the state-based nationalists of the Persians, Turks and Arabs that are dominant nations with all rights.

Arab, Turkish, Persian and Kurdish nationalism

According to the above-mentioned definition of nation and nationalism, in the Middle East and around Kurdistan there are different nationalisms and several "nationalistic confrontations" between Arab, Turkish, Persian/Iranian and Kurdish nationalists. With the weakening of the multi-national Ottoman Caliphate under the domination of the Turks, and the tendency of the state towards centralization and the development of nationalist movements all over the Ottoman realm, in the late nineteenth - early twentieth century, Turkish nationalism appeared to preserve the interests of the Turkish nation based on a Turkish version of the theory of Turanism; purifying, strengthening the Turanian/Turkish race and unifying the relevant peoples (see: Stoddard, 1917). The main element of Turkish nationalism is Turkish ethnicity, language and culture. At the beginning of the advent of a Turkish state (1918-24) and during the early years of the twenty-first century, Turkish nationalism further used religion. In Turkey, there was an aggressive conflict between Turkish and Kurdish nationalists during the last century which continues today.

The beginnings of Arab nationalism, like Turkish or others, can be traced back to the last decades of nineteenth century (1880s) and even the activities of Christian intellectuals, a time when the impact of European thinking was at its highest point in the Middle East (Breuilly, 1993, 150; Hastings, 1999, 201). Nevertheless, its deep ethno-religious roots emerged with the advent of Islam and then Arabization through the Arabic language as the Islamic sacred language. Its main elements include Arabic ethnicity and language, Islam and Islamic culture. Although most Arab nationalists are secular and some of them non-Muslim, they see Islam as an important factor in Arab nationalism and have used it in favour of their interests (Mofidi, 2015a, 48). Indeed, Islam has served Arabic ethnicity, language and culture throughout history, as well as Arab nationalism in the modern age. The Arab nationalist movement resulted in many Arabic states being formed with few differences, so that the common factors have often made a ground for their unity. Arab nationalists in Syria and Iraq have had confrontations with Kurdish nationalists.

Almost simultaneously with the changes in the Ottoman Empire, by weakening the Qajar non-centralized kingdom and the first revolution (Constitutional R.) in 1905, the Iranian/Persian nationalism emerged to pursue the interests of a Persian/Fars nation in this multinational country. Persian nationalists used the word 'Iran' to extend the scope of their nationalism and show the nations/ethnicities as part of the Iranian nation, however only the Persian identity was emphasized. Thus, Iranian nationalism was the equivalent of Persian/Fars ethno-nationalism, with its main pillars being Persian/Farsi ethnicity, language, culture and Shiite religion. Persian nationalists have followed the motto of 'One Nation, One Language, and One Country' (Mohammadpour and Soleimani, 2020). After the 1979 revolution, the Persian nationalists increasingly used religion to serve their nationalistic aims. There has been confrontation between Perso-Iranian nationalists and other nationalists including Kurds, Turks, Turkmens, Balouchs and Arabs in Iran.

The above-mentioned nationalisms are indeed state nationalisms, based on the ethno-nationalism of a dominant ethno-nation. As Hakan Yavuz (2007) mentions, the important difference between them and Kurdish nationalism "is the presence of the state". Kurdish nationalism is a sub-state nationalism based on a nation without a state. The genesis of modern Kurdish national identity[4] is related to 'the relationship

---

[4] About the political, historical, territorial and linguistic identities of Kurds see: Hassanpour (2003, pp. 106-162).

of the self and other with the emergent Turkish, Persian and Arab identities in the early decades of the twenty century'(Vali, 2003, 104). The main elements and pillars of the Kurdish nation are Kurdish ethnicity, language[5], culture and territory that have tied the Kurdish people to each other. Even research shows that there is an individual solidarity among Kurds as 'imagined community' (Akbarzadeh et al., 2019). Thus, by most definitions of nation whether based on common mentioned criteria or others, like having a sense of social group or an imagination of themselves, Kurds are mostly considered as a nation by scholars. According to Abbas Vali (2003), the concept of Kurdish nationalism refers to "the multiplicity of discourses and practices which define the Kurds as a uniform nation with sovereign rights to their homeland, Greater Kurdistan" (p. 58). This long socio-political movement has been seeking self-determination to gain human rights for the Kurds and equality with other nations. The political actors of this nation play an important role in the political arena of the Middle East.

In the four above-mentioned countries, Kurdish nationalism seeks the political rights of the Kurdish nation and others seek the interests of dominant nations. Indeed, the nationalism of dominant state nationalists has gone beyond the nationalist wishes towards chauvinism. They have not regarded the rights of the sub-state or stateless nations and have been trying to assimilate other ethno-nations by practising "various forms of ethnocide, linguicide and genocide" (Hassanpour, 2003, 107). In these confrontations, based on their abilities both sides have used different ways and means including the political function of religion to gain their nationalistic aims.

---

[5] According to Ghassemlou (1993), "Kurdish language and literature have contributed to the consolidation of national feeling" (p. 98). About the effect of language on creating nations and nationalism, see: Hastings (1999, pp. 11-12).

Figure 1. The nationalistic confrontations in Kurdistan

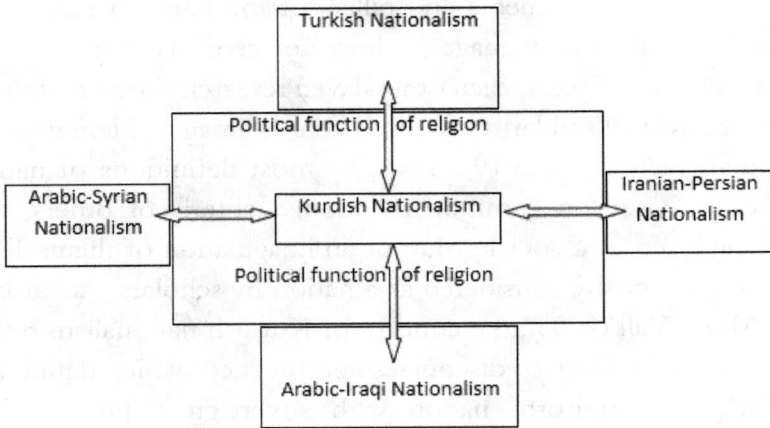

NATIONALISTIC CONFRONTATIONS IN CONTEMPORARY KURDISTAN

During the modern age, Kurds have seen Kurdistan as a colony[1], an internal colony by relevant states, which needs to be freed. There have been three phases of Kurdish movements in Kurdistan: the principalities' revolts, religious figures' uprising, and political parties' activities. In the nineteenth century, the principalities' revolts petitioning for the creation of a Kurdish state were suppressed by the Ottoman Empire, often under the name of religion and the symbol of the Caliphate. Nevertheless, although making an independent state was not possible for different nations including the Kurds, some equal rights of citizenship were granted during the Islamic period until the last decades of the Ottoman Empire, when they were affected by the advent of the pan-Islamism of Sultan Abdulhamid II (1876-1908) and the emergence of Pan-Turkism especially against the Czar's pan-Slavism, and also the effect of Arab nationalism (Bruinessen, 1992, 269). Muslim Arab revivalist nationalists such as Abd al-Rahman al-Kawakibi (1855-1902) reinterpreted Islamic concepts in favour of Arab nationalism. For them Islam and Arabs were not separable. Against the Ottoman Turks who tried to preserve their empire's integrity, the Arabs refused an Islamic Umma/nation (Muslim community) and focused on Islamic Umam/nations in which the Arab Umma was the most important (See: Soleimani, 2018). Then, in reaction to the pan-

---

[1] Even some Kurdish and non-Kurdish mixed groups have supported the thesis of Kurdistan's status as a colony. For example, the *Kurtuluş* movement (Emancipation movement), a communist organization in Turkey in the 1970s, of which Dersim became its stronghold, can be mentioned (see: Deniz, 2020; Orhan, 2016).

Turkist policies of the Young Turks (1908-1914), Muslim Arab and Kurdish intellectuals further developed their nationalist awareness (Maóz, 1999, 12). Almost simultaneously in Iran, also in reaction to the development of pan-Farsist policies especially from the time Reza Shah came to power (1925) and the forming a quasi-modern centralized state[2], the different ethno-nationalisms, especially Kurdish nationalism, grew.

At the end of the nineteenth and early in the twentieth century the two characteristics of Kurdish society were its tribal nature and its religiosity (Barkey and Fuller, 1998, 65). So, in line with other Muslim nations and their states' use of religion, the Kurds also tried to use religion to create their own state. This occurred during the religious figures' uprisings, especially those of the Tarighat sheikhs and their families, who used their influence in society; for example, the unsuccessful movements of Sheikh Ubeydullah, Sheikh Said Barzinja, Sheikh Mahmud, Sheikh Said Piran, Sheikh Riza, Sheikh Salam Barzani, Mela Mustafa and Qazi Muhammed. Sheikh Ubeydullah's nationalist project in 1880 against the Ottoman and Qajar Turks was one example of the fusion of Islam with nationalism among Islamic nations which started in the nineteenth century. In an interview with American missionary Henry Otis Dwight in 1881, he tried to show that the Turkish and Persian leaders of dominant nations had no real faith and only use it politically (Soleimani, 2018).

After Sheikh Ubeydullah's revolt, the formation of Hamidiye Cavalry Regiments[3] and the pretext of the threat of war with non-Muslim Russia led to weakening of the Kurdish movement. After 1909, when the Young Turks and Unionists came to power, the Committee of Union and Progress (CUP)

---

[2] Because of the lack of some of the criteria of Modern States it is called 'quasi-modern state' by the author (For more details See: Mofidi and Rahmani, 2018).

[3] A special Kurdish force among the tribes created by Sultan Abdulhamid II (1876-1909) in 1891 which were composed of Kurds, while all ranks above colonel were assigned to the Turks (Mofidi, 2021; White, 2000, 60)

government closed or suppressed several Kurdish societies in Istanbul, Baghdad and Mosul, as well as several journals in Istanbul. The CUP adopted a new centralization policy, with the clear aim of imposing Turkish culture and language throughout the empire, and the non-religious features of the new Ottoman constitution were observed. These measures led to opposition from Sheikh Said Barzinji, leader of the Qadiri order in Silêmanî (Sulaimani), in 1909, and subsequently his deportation to Mosul. In the same year, he was killed in a conspiracy, during a major clash in Mosul while negotiating with the government. Then, his son, Sheikh Mahmoud, returned to Silêmanî. He had the support of the Hamawand tribe which by 1914 was still not suppressed (Fieldhouse, 2001, 36 & 164). Along with some Arab Sheikhs, Sheikh Mahmoud fought against Britain in 1914-1915. After the defeat of the Ottoman governors of Baghdad and Basra by the British, he filled the political vacuum in Southern Kurdistan in Iraq (hereafter Başûr/Bashur). From 1918, along with Sheikh Mahmoud's struggles in Başûr, Kurdish dissention continued in Northern Kurdistan in Turkey (hereafter Bakûr), which after the collapse of the Ottoman Caliphate and establishment of the Turkish state led to the uprising of Sheikh Said of Piran and its suppression in 1925. Subsequently, the Kurdish movement continued, often under the leadership of other religious figures.

From the second half of the twentieth century, the third stage of the Kurdish movement started, with the Kurdish parties and their leaders often leading the movement in the four parts of Kurdistan. Nevertheless, the secular nationalists considered religion as a means of gaining people's support, especially Sunnis who, according to Bruinessen (2000), have often formed the backbone of the Kurdish movement. Thus, after the destruction of the Kurdish principalities there were many revolts, sometimes resulting in short-term Kurdish control of parts of Kurdistan; the self-proclaimed states of Sheikh Ubeydullah (1880-1) and Simko

(1918-22), reign of Sheikh Mahmoud (1920s), Kurdistan Republic (1946), Kurdish autonomy in Bashûr (1970-1974), Kurdish parties' control of part of Eastern Kurdistan in Iran (hereafter Rojhelat) after the 1979 Iranian revolution, the Kurdistan Regional Government (KRG) in Bashûr (1991-) and eventually self-administration in Western Kurdistan in Syria (hereafter Rojava) (2013-).

The impact of the above political changes in the Middle East and the continuity of the Kurdish movement, was long-term nationalistic confrontation. After World War I, the collapse of the Ottoman Caliphate and Qajar dynasty, then the formation of new states, in the four countries overlapping Kurdistan the dominant ethno-nationalists and the Kurds have relentlessly confronted each other. "The Kurds are othered by the stronger and more nationalistic or religiously-organized nations the Turks, Arabs and Persians" (Dehzani, 2008, 4).[4] Although among the four countries only the Iranian government is currently religious, all states have used religion in favour of their politics against the Kurdish national movement, as examined in the following sections.

---

[4] Although in these countries some Kurds without reference to their original ethnicity have participated in political systems, such as the two presidents of Syria in the 1950s, some Kurds in the Ba'ath cabinet in Iraq, and some in the Turkish and Iranian governments, like Bijan Zangeneh, who many times became the oil minister of the Islamic Republic of Iran. But the Kurds have not considered them as the representatives of their collective identity in the political sphere and even see them as servants of the dominant ethno-nations. Their presence in the systems have not even been a kind of tokenism, accepting the others' ethnicity they have not identified themselves as Kurdish.

TURKEY: TURKISH-KURDISH
CONFRONTATION IN BAKÛR

In the Ottoman Empire the Kurds were one nation among many in a multi-national polity. Until the nineteenth century they had their own principalities and afterwards their situation as Muslim was not so bad. In the empire, under Ottoman Islamic law minorities were defined by religion not ethnicity. Although gradually in the centralizing process the Kurdish autonomous principalities were removed, the Sunni majority of Kurds had influence in the caliphate. As Kedourie (1992) mentions "Islam was the dominant element in this polity, and as Muslims, Kurds felt at home in it" (p. 289). Along with Turks and Arabs, the Kurds were the Muslim socio-religious core of the empire. At least linguistically and culturally they didn't have a problem (Barkey and Fuller, 1998, 3-6).

However, the Alevi Kurds, as non-Sunni and even non-Muslim[1], had a problem. The Ottoman rulers and the Sunni theologians denounced Alevis as heretics and infidels (Vorhoff, 2003, 94). Although between the seventeenth and the end of nineteenth century the situation of the Alevis improved, from the reign of Abdulhamid II (1876-1909), under his new politics of Islamism, their status worsened and some were compulsorily assimilated and converted. The Hamidiye Cavalry attacked the Alevis and confiscated their lands (Kehl-Bodrogi, 2003, 56). This

---

[1] Alevi (also known as Qizilbash) Kurds have mysticism and Ali, the first Shia Imam and fourth Sunni Caliph, is a most important personage for them. The present Alevism in Bakûr is similar to Kakeiy in Başûr or Yarsan/Ahl-I Hagh/Ali-u-Allahi in Rojhelat, an indigenous Kurdish religion, which are syncretic religions and pseudo-Islam. Although they have some aspects of Shia Islam, they are not accepted as Muslim by both Sunnis and Shias (Keles, 2014; Mofidi, 2021).

increased sectarianism among the Kurds and triggered many other setbacks in future Kurdish politics in favour of the Turks. In addition to the Alevis' opposition to the Ottoman Empire and Islamist politics, the traditional antagonism of Alevi Kurds towards the Empire contained a Kurdish element because they lost their recognized autonomy from 1839, especially in Dersim, by instigating Tanzimat (reforms), although they preserved the region autonomously through some local powers until 1937. So, Alevis who in the Ottoman period were neither protected as a minority nor accepted within the Islamic Umma, hoped to gain a better situation and equality in the young Turkey than they had had in the past. In supporting secularism against the Caliphate and Sultan Abdulhamid's despotism, they had sympathized with the Young Turks and CUP, then with Ataturk and the Kemalists, who portrayed themselves as secularist and freedom-fighters. The Turks changed their politics to the Alevis and the transformed state recalled the militia from Dersim (Kehl-Bodrogi, 2003, 56-60; Kieser, 2003, 177-9; Vorhoff, 2003, 94). Nevertheless, the political change did not serve to foster religious pluralism. They were, therefore, still concerned about the dangers of assimilation, since based on Turkish nationalist theory, especially that of Ziya Gokalp[2], the same language and the same religion were the pillars of the nation (Keiser, 2003, 180).

At the end of the Ottoman period, the Turks used the conflict between Islam and other religions to reinforce the integrity of the empire and the Kurds were sacrificed to this religious cleavage (See: Bozarsalan, 2003c, 171-182). The experience of the war between the Russian and Ottoman governments and the unity of the Armenians and Russians to motivate the Armenian inhabitants in the eastern provinces against the Ottomans in 1915 (Macfie, 1998, 132), provided an

---

[2] Ziya Gokalp, one of the leading contributors to Turkish nationalism, was an assimilated Kurd from Diyarbakir (Olson, 1989, 16).

opportunity for the Turks to use the religious conflict to attract the Kurds under Jihad against non-Muslims during World War I and the Independence War. Thus, by instigation of the Turks' pan-Islamic propaganda during the wars the Sunni Kurds were deceived and remained generally loyal to the Ottomans (ibid., 213), while the Alevis feared suffering the same fate as the Armenians in 1915. This unsettled the Unionists because of a possible political alliance between Alevi Kurds and Christian Armenians. Seyid Reza[3], religious leader of the Alevi Kurds, did not help the Ottomans to make Alevi Kurds in Dersim participate in the Jihad. Against the expectation of the Ottoman general staff, they didn't fight against the Russians in 1915. They helped the Armenians and offered them their services and hospitality. They rebelled in favour of Kurdish nationalism to gain independence in 1916. Some of the Kurdish nationalists who mistrusted the Turks also tried to use the enmity of Alevis and pan-Islamists (Bozarsalan, 2003a, 9; Kieser, 2003, 179-183). With the development of the revolt of Dersim, however, the Ottomans used the religious sentiments of Sunni Kurds in Harput against a coordinated Kurdish-Russian advance to crush the revolt (Keiser, 2003, 183).

After WWI, in the last years of the Ottoman Caliphate and the early years of Turkish Republic, Turkish politicians used religion to influence the Kurdish forces. Indeed, in what was called the residue of the Empire and 'Ottoman Muslims', Turkish nationalists appealed to them to resist in 1919, including the Turks and the Kurds (Howard, 2017, 314). Following the establishment of the Turkish national movement, its leaders used Islamic sentiments to attract Kurdish people to repel foreign forces, launching a propaganda campaign emphasizing the threat of invasion of an independent Christian Armenia on Kurdistan,

---

[3] Seyid/Seyt (Seyyid) Reza/Riza was an Alevi cleric who then supported the 1921 Kochgiri revolt and led the 1937 Dersim revolt.

and collapse of the Caliphate institution by the Allies as a sacred symbol for the Muslim Kurds controlling Istanbul. They identified it as the war of Muslims against non-Muslim invaders and communities. Both Kemalist and pro-Sultan forces propagated against Bolshevism as an anti-religious ideology that would bring an "end to the family, to religion, to all morality" (Nezan, 1993b, 205). Moreover, presenting themselves as the defenders of all Muslims against western invaders, they supported the Kurdish opposition against Britain in Başûr (See: Bozarsalan, 2003c, 181). So under Muslim fraternity, attracting Kurdish elites they encouraged Kurds to fight to escape domination by the Armenians and for the creation of a Muslim state under the spiritual authority of the Caliph. The Turkish nationalists used this anti-Christian Armenian fear especially at the Erzrum congress, July 23 to August 6, 1919 to facilitate a Kurdish-Turkish alliance. In the congress fifty-four delegates from the five Kurdish vilayets were threatened with annexation of their vilayets to Armenia. The congress decided to prevent Armenia annexing Muslim territories and to liberate the Muslim lands occupied by the infidels. In the second congress at Sivas in September 1919, representatives from all over Turkey focused on the integration of the Islamic parts of the Ottoman Empire. Consequently, about 70 Kurdish representatives, as shareholders in the Muslim patrimony, supported Mustafa Kemal (Ataturk), a Turkish officer, to lead the independence movement. In the name of the Muslims of Anatolia, he revolted against Christian forces; Greeks, Armenians and Soviets supported by the infidel Western powers (Bozarsalan, 2003c, 171-172; Bruinessen, 1992, 272; Macfie, 1998, 195; McDowall, 1992, 17-18; Nezan, 1993, 46-47; Romano, 2006, 104). Ataturk gained the Sunni majority's support by covering his secularist aims and emphasizing the preservation of the Caliphate and the Islamic character of the struggle as a Holy War (Kehl-Bodrogi, 2003, 58). Promoting

Islam as an inspiration for his forces, he urged Turkish and Kurdish unity in the struggle to liberate the Muslim Fatherland (Gourlay, 2020). According to Nezan (1993), Ataturk in Kurdish territory "presented himself as the savior of Kurdistan, the champion of a Caliph imprisoned by the occupation forces and the defender of the Muslim lands soiled by the impious Christians" (p. 46). In his letters to Kurdish sheikhs, Ataturk warned them about the ineptitude of the Caliph and the Istanbul government and the annexing of Kurdish Vilayets to Armenia (Olson, 1989, 37-38). By these measures, he turned the minds of Kurdish leaders to the conflict between Muslim and non-Muslim, and prevented their support of Kurdish nationalist claims and the Kochgiri revolt (Olson, 1989, 38). Instead, during the War of Independence (1919-1923) under the power of Kurds and their support for the Caliph, both the Istanbul government and Kemalist leaders promised to recognize Kurdish political entity within the future state. In the Treaty of Sèvres signed by the Allies and Turkish government on August 10, 1920, section III (article 62-64), the rights of Kurds for self-determination was recognized, whether in the form of an independent or an autonomous Kurdish state (Nezan, 1993, 48). Nevertheless, as Bozarsalan (2003c) shows, under the name of Islam and the caliphate the Kurdish forces were divided, so that some of them defended a Kurdish state, and others autonomy renewing the Kurdish-Turkish fraternity. This resulted in weakening and marginalizing Kurdish nationalism during the war of independence.

Conversely, although Ataturk had a plan for creating a broad front including Alevis and other non-Christian communities, he was not able to attract the majority of Alevi Kurds[4] in the war

---

[4] Alevi Kurds also known as Dimilis, Dimli-Zazas, Dersimlis and Kizilbash. Dimilis are attributed to Dailamite. According to some scholars like Mehrdad Izady, Dailamites were originally from Kurdistan but some of them reached North of today's Iran called also Dailam (Paul, 2003, 21).

because of the existence of the Caliphate and a majority of his Sunni supporters. The Alevis feared the same fate as the Armenians. Nevertheless, along with pan-Islamist discourse under which letters had been sent to Kurdish sheikhs, Ataturk succeeded in gaining some Alevi chieftains and officers as deputies, though only as marginal elements in the Ankara Kemalist Assembly (Bozarsalan, 2003a, 8-9). This damaged the unity of the Alevi Kurds. Despite this, skirmishes between Turks and Kurds took place in early 1921. In fact, in 1919 the Society for the Rise of Kurdistan (KTC)[5] headed by Sheikh Abdulqadir, the son of Sheikh Ubeydullah, with some leaders from the Alevi region, based on US President Wilson's Fourteen Points[6] and the principle of self-determination for individual nations, tried to outline the establishment of an independent Kurdistan, which affected the Alevi region (Keiser, 2003, 185; White, 2000, 68-71). At the time, Ataturk invited the leaders of the Kochgiri-Dersim people to the Sivas congress. Alishan, their representative, demanded Kurdish autonomy within an Ottoman federation. The congress took no notice of the demand. Indeed, Ataturk had verbally promised autonomy, but after attracting the support of the majority of Sunnis to the Kemalist movement, especially under the pretext of countering non-Muslims, he neglected his promise and Alevi Kurds were marginalized. Then, in solidarity with the Kurdish nationalists and Alevi members of KTC like Mehmet Nuri Dersimi and Alisher[7], after the Treaty of Sèvres in 1920, following Wilson's principles the Alevi Kurds tried to use the conditions to attain self-determination (Kieser, 2003, 184-7).

---

[5] Kurdistan Taali Cemeyeti, founded in 1918, was different from Kurdistan Taali ve Terakki Cemeyeti (KTTC).

[6] Ironically the twelfth point of Woodrow Wilson's plan during WWI directly concerned the Kurds which was about self-determination for individual nations and granting the right of 'autonomous development' for non-Turkish minorities of the Ottoman Empire (Barkey and Fuller, 1998, 204; Dehzani, 2008, 64; Gunter, 2011, 4).

[7] A chief agitator in the Kurdish Alevi independence movement who was in contact with Abdulqadir.

They first demanded Kurdish autonomy for all of Kurdistan, regardless of religious affiliation, then local autonomy for their districts (Bruinessen, 1992, 52). When they did not receive a reasonable response to their 5-point declaration presented to the Kemalist government in Ankara, they generally refused to cooperate with Ataturk and agitated against the Kemalist movement (Olson, 1989, 26). This led to the Kochgiri revolt led by Alishan Beg and supported by Seyid Reza[8] in 1920-21 when they demanded their right to self-determination based on their Kurdishness (Kieser, 2003, 185). Nevertheless, it was not successful against Ataturk's policy and was perceived by Sunni Kurds as an Alevi uprising (White, 2000, 86).

At the time, in the Dersim area the old conflict between Alevi and Sunni, as well as Hamidiye and non-Hamidiye tribes reemerged (Olson, 1989, 26-32). The politics of Ataturk towards Alevi Kurds and Turks were different. He had an ethnic connection with the Alevi Turks and could attract most of them, but there was no common element with the Alevi Kurds. While simultaneously Alevi Turks like Sunnis, in the name of national defence, supported Ataturk, he was at war with Alevi Kurds who at that time were supporters of Kurdish nationalism. Some Sunni Kurdish nationalists at the beginning also supported the movement of Alevi Kurds against Ataturk, while the Turks needed the Sunni Kurdish forces. So, Ataturk used the Islamist sentiments of the Sunni majority, especially by appealing to the Kurds' Islamic Identity and their religious sectarianism, to counter and suppress the Kochgiri uprising. Thus, the majority of Kurds supported Ataturk and the Kochgiri rebels remained isolated (see, Bozarsalan, 2003a, 10; Bozarsalan, 2003c, 174; Kehl-Bodrogi, 2003, 60; Olson, 1989; Romano, 2006, 28 & 104). Nevertheless, after the Kemalist forces' suppression of the

---

[8] He was from Abbasushagi tribe but supported the revolt of Kochgiri tribes.

Kochgiri revolt, Ataturk again used secularism to attract Alevis.

In 1922, Ataturk finally overcame the Istanbul government, which had signed the Treaty of Sèvres, and declared a Turkish state (Macfie, 1998, 195; Vanely, 1993, 146). When Ataturk fully seized power, he stood against the rights of the Kurds. In the beginning, his intentions for the nascent state remained hidden, he still allowed the Kurds to join the Kemalists under the auspices of saving the Ottoman legacy in a state based on Turkish-Kurdish brotherhood and equality. In his own words, "Turks and Kurds will continue to live together as brothers around the institution of the Caliphate" (Romano, 2006, 30). Accordingly, Turkish nationalist delegations imposed a Turkish nation at the Lausanne Conference on 24 July 1923, using religion to hide and marginalize the Kurdish question and to remove the ethno-national rights of Kurds. As a result, only non-Muslims were regarded as a minority (Gunter, 2011, 99; Kendal, 1993, 34 & 51; Macfie, 1998, 207). Thus, marginalizing Kurdish nationalism during these years by appealing to Islamic identity, suppression and secularism by Turks, prevented the formation of a Kurdish political entity. Consequently, with the abolition of the Caliphate, the Kurds rose up against the secular state "in both a Kurdish nationalist and a religious light" (Romano, 2006, 105).

Religious Kurds vs. secular Turkish state (1923-1937)

Unlike under the Ottoman Empire, in the secular Republic of Turkey citizenship was closely connected with Turkishness. The regime attempted to remove Kurdish identity and repressed Kurdish revolts in the 1920s and 1930s (Kedourie, 1992, 289). The short-lived Turkish Constitution of 1921 based on Wilson's points and the Treaty of Sèvres had included autonomy for the Kurds. Ignoring international law and human rights, the Kemalists hid the rights of Kurds under being Muslim. While the Kemalists rejected the Sèvres configuration, the Treaty of

Lausanne could be read as including the Kurds. But it was not implemented (see: Pentassuglia, 2020). Thus, the Turkish nationalists tried to assimilate the Kurds. However, in the period between 1924 and 1990, the secular government rarely used religion against the Kurdish nationalists, instead it deployed military force to suppress them. Conversely, some Kurdish leaders like Sheikh Said Piran and Seyid Reza of Dersim rebelled, using their religious influence in Kurdish society. From the 1990s when Islamic forces gradually came to power, the regime again increasingly used religion against the Kurdish movement. Although Islamic parties like the Refah/Welfare Party (RP), founded in 1983, and the Justice and Development Party (JDP/AKP), founded in 2001, used the legacy of the Ottoman Empire and developed an 'Islamic formula' to face the Kurdish forces without offending Turkish nationalism, they were unable to present an alternative providing ethno-national rights to the Kurds (Barkey and Fuller, 1998, 4).

At the end of the Caliphate, the Sunni Kurds still had some socio-cultural liberties and felt there was Muslim fraternity. But the abolition of a common caliphate was the end of that bond and for Kurdish leaders it meant Turkish repression. However, the Kurds tied themselves to the symbol of the Caliphate which was regarded as "the source of Kurdish resistance", in Bozarsalan's words (2003c, 179). The abolition of the Caliphate, secularizing reforms, omitting the name of "Kurdistan" in all educational and geographical books, and banning all Kurdish organizations and newspapers as well as the use of the Kurdish language in public places, under the constitution of 1924, provided grounds for another Kurdish revolt supported by nationalist Kurds including political, religious and military forces (Olson, 1989, 44, 91 & 153). Then, the previous Sunni Kurdish supporters of the Kemalists rose up against them and Kurdish army officers of the Hamidiye regiment became key supporters and leaders of the political organization Azadi (Freedom Committee/Civata Azadiya Kurd established in 1923), which incited a Kurdish uprising. In contrast, the Kemalists dismissed any Kurdish opposition as feudalist and a religious reaction against secular progress (Kieser, 2003, 189). Although, rather than in the time of Shaikh Ubeydullah, nationalist forces had grown further, the leadership was still in the hands of religious figures and the challenge of secularism led to more order within the religious organizations in Kurdistan. The Azadi took advantage of Naqshbandi order, the traditional position of its sheikhs and their attraction, appeal and reputation among the Kurdish population. The Naqshbandi sheikhs became the most important leaders of the revolt. The most famous Sheikh and primarily a nationalist with many followers, Said of Piran, was one of the most outspoken nationalists in the first Azadi congress in 1924 (Olson, 1989, 92-101, 114 and 153). The political leaders selected him as general leader and employed his religious charisma and influence in order to mobilize the masses in 1925 (Bruinessen, 1992, 265-66; Romano, 2006, 34). Although the secularism of the Young Turks and then Ataturk had affected the ideological stance of Sheikh Said, according to some scholars, his revolt was a nationalist movement in a religious dress (Olson, 1989, 153). The uprising had both nationalistic and religious characters. It was another Kurdish national movement with its leadership against the secularist and anti-Islamic tendencies of the new regime in Turkey (Barkey and Fuller, 1998, 11). Sheikh Said used the opportunity and the "religious and ethnic fervour" (Zaki, 1931, 257) to rise up against the new secular Republic before it became more stable, in order to create an independent Muslim Kurdish state, as well as symbolically reinstituting the Caliphate (Gunter, 2011, 100). Sheikh Said's utterance, in a handwritten letter attributed to him, that: "Under the pretext of religion and the Caliphate, the Turks and the Ottomans have for over 400 years been pushing us gradually towards slavery, darkness, ignorance and destruction. [...] They came among us as migrants. [...]" (quoted by: Bozarsalan, 2003c, 176), shows that the Kurdish religious leaders became aware that the Turks had used Islamic symbols and sentiments in favour of their nationalist aims, so they tried to do the same.

Although religion was not a motivation for many of the initiators of Sheikh Said's rebellion, it was a major mobilizing factor for the masses and most of its combatants (White, 2000, 74). Indeed, at that time, under the effect of the abolition of the caliphate, religious agitation was more effective in gaining mass support than nationalist propaganda alone. Thus, the Kurdish nationalists considered the political function of religion to religiously justify their nationalist movement (see: Bruinessen, 1992, 298). They might even have considered reconstituting the Islamic Caliphate under a Kurdish caliph or Kurdish state by using Muslim sentiments. For Sheikh Said, Islam was the basis of unity that had been betrayed by the Turks. He proclaimed that Muslims should overthrow the Turkish Republic and Ataturk as they were hostile to the Quran, God, the Prophet and Caliphate (Bozarsalan, 2003c, 180-184). As for the Kemalist government, he denounced it for destroying religion and issued a fatwa, declaring the rebellion against it lawful. In his speeches he denounced the Turkish politicians and their godless policies. As leader of the Naqshbandi order, he mobilized the masses and declared himself the "representative of the Caliph and of Islam." Sheikh Said claimed a kind of Naqshbandi Caliphate. In the name of religion, he asked the people and the Kurdish chieftains to join the revolt in a holy war (Jihad), becoming a holy fighter (Mujahid) against Ankara's secular government. He took the title of Amir al-mujahidin (commander of the warriors of holy war) and his forces carried the Quran next to their bayonets. In their attacks against the Kemalist regime, the sheikh's forces chanted Islamic slogans like "Praises to God!"(Olson, 1989, 94-109). Nevertheless, resorting to religion and the caliphate at the beginning of secularism in Turkey did not work out for the Kurds. The regime presented the Kurdish movement to the outside world as "a reactionary religious revolt geared to re-establish the Caliphate and the Ottoman dynasty" (Nezan, 1993, 54), while it repressed the movement, and sentenced and executed Kurdish forces because of their attempt to constitute an independent Kurdistan. Meanwhile, the Turkish Kemalist politicians themselves established a state based not only on the Turkish identity that emerged at the end of the nineteenth century (Jongerden, 2003, 75) but also, according to Hamit Bozarsalan, Turkish Islamic Synthesis, an ideology rooted in the ideas of Ziya Gökalp between 1910 and 1920, as the official ideology of Turkey (Deniz, 2020).

During Sheikh Said's uprising, religious sectarianism and sectarian politics were again used by Turkish politicians to counter his revolt. Against the Kurdish nationalists supported by Sunni Kurds, by changing his strategy Ataturk used secularism to silence the Alevi Kurds and to attract their support for a secular Turkey (Kehl-Bodrogi, 2003, 60). Turkish politicians scared the Alevi Kurdish people with the image of an independent Kurdistan under the authority of Sunni Sheikhs, and promised them that the secular state of Turkey would secure their equal rights. Whilst, as mentioned, they had already suppressed the Alevi Kurds' Kochgiri revolt in 1921, the secular state again suppressed their popular resistance movement in 1937 (Bruinessen, 1992, 294). Ataturk used hidden methods to mobilize the Alevis. He tried to use the fear of the dangers of religious identity against the Alevis' ethnic identity. Ataturk by abolishing the caliphate, dissolving Sharia courts and the office of the Sheikh-ul-Islam between 1922 and 1924, eliminated the institutional obstacles to the Alevis' equality with the Sunni majority, regarding them as part of the Islamic population and national resistance. He appealed to them especially through their tribal and religious chiefs. These measures let to the mythologizing of Ataturk by all Turkish and Kurdish Alevis. He was considered as Mehdi and saviour (see: Kehl-Bodrogi, 2003, 57-62). Alevis considered Kemalist programme as a political project to end the Sunni domination over them and moving towards them being legally equal citizens (Jongerden, 2003, 82). Moreover, their fear of the religious tone of the revolt and the presence of old Hamidiye commanders among the Sheikh's forces was effective. The already-mentioned Ottoman Hamidiye cavalry, composed of Sunni Kurds, in the late nineteenth century had been used against the Alevis (Kieser, 2003, 190; White, 2000, 75 & 80). Thus, the Turkish politicians succeeded in their political aspirations and the majority of Alevi Kurds distanced themselves from the movement. They did not support the Kurdish uprising of 1925 and formation of a Sunni-led independent Kurdistan, although some Alevi deputies joined Sheikh Said, like Hasan Hayri who was later executed by the regime (Bozarsalan, 2003a, 8). Supporting Kemalism, some Alevi tribes like the Khurmak and Lawlan actively opposed and fought against the movement. So, the Kurdish nationalists simultaneously fought the Turkish government and Alevi Kurds as the government's agents, directly or indirectly, who were against the Kurdish fighters (See: Bruinessen, 1992, 52; Bruinessen, 1996; Bruinessen, 1999; Bruinessen, 2000; Olson, 1989, 94; Romano, 2006, 34). During the war, a number of the Kurdish forces were killed by Alevis in Dersim (Olson, 1989, 110).

Gradually, under the Kemalist programme, the aims of the regime were revealed. In the 1927 rubric of the single Kemalist party, the unity of language, feelings and thoughts were emphasized for its given nation (Kieser, 2003, 190). This led to a continuation of the Kurdish revolts by both Sunnis and Alevis.

Nevertheless, the religious divisions within Kurdish society again affected them negatively. The Mount Ararat/Agri revolt under Ihsan Nouri Pasha, a former Sunni supporter of the Caliphate, mostly had Sunni Kurdish support, with just a few Alevi tribes joining it, although its leader was not a religious figure. Finally, the revolt was crushed in 1930. (Romano, 2006, 107; White, 2000, 76-7; White, 2003, 24). Similarly, in the Dersim (Tunceli) revolt (1937-8), supported mostly by Alevi Kurds, another failure ensued.

From the beginning of the 1930s onwards the Kemalist regime attacked the Alevi Kurds of Dersim, the last autonomous region in Kurdistan (Kieser, 2003, 191). This time the Kurdish revolt was headed by an Alevi cleric, Seyid Reza, the most important spiritual and political leader. He insisted upon autonomy but eventually on 10 September 1937 surrendered (ibid., 192-3). This time the Sunni Kurds were silent and turned away from the revolt, even though it had a Kurdish nationalist character. Nevertheless, the secular state did not use the religious justification openly. Instead, it used other methods against Kurdish nationalism. It suppressed the Kurdish uprising by battling against backwardness and feudalism (Kehl-Bodrogi, 2003, 66). Indeed, the regime's discourse and military operations in Dersim, 1937-38, were used primarily to implement the policies of Turkification and Islamization which denied Kurdish ethnicity and targeted Alevi religion. To remove Kurdishness, the Turks treated Dersim as a colony.[9] Because of the religious influence of the Alevi Seyids, members of an important Alevi institution in the society, the state targeted them as a danger among Alevi Kurds. The main Alevi Seyid families, especially of that of Seyid Reza, were among those specifically targeted for

---

[9] The Commander of General of Staff, Mustafa Fevzi Çakmak (1876-1950), at the time of the suppression of Dersim had said: "Dersim should primarily be accepted as a colony, Kurdishness should be melted into Turkishness, and then should be subjected to particular Turkish jurisdiction" (Deniz, 2020).

killing and exile (Deniz, 2020). Before his death, Seyid Reza fuelled Kurdish nationalism with some religious sentiments. For him the murdered Kurdish combatants were the martyrs of Kurdistan, whom the Kurdish youth should revenge (White, 2000, 83). According to some scholars such as Deniz (2020), the suppression of the 1937-38 revolt in Dersim was genocide.

However, the religion-based political ramifications of the Sunni-Alevi division affected the new Kurdish nationalism so that the Alevi Kurds were betrayed in the Kochgiri revolt by Sunni Kurds who cooperated with the Caliphate. The Sunni Kurds were betrayed in Sheikh Said's revolt by Alevi Kurds who cooperated with the new secular Republic state, and again in the Dersim revolt Alevi Kurds were not supported by Sunni Kurds (Barkey and Fuller, 1998, 69). Thus, during this transitional period, the Turkish state and nationalists used the religious cleavages in Kurdistan to advance their politics. When the centre of the Kurdish revolt was in the Alevi area, they tried to suppress them under an Alevi revolt to keep the Sunni Kurds silent, and vice versa.

On the other hand, after the Caliphate the Turkish nationalists also used Islam as a homogenized religion to cover ethno-national cleavages between the Turks and Kurds in favour of Turkish nationalism. They used "the abandonment of the Ottoman legacy, and of Islam as the spiritual soul of the newborn Turkish Republic" (Bozarsalan, 2003c, 179). So, Ataturk first used Islam and announced Turkey as a Muslim country to cover the ethnic cleavages and suppress the Kurdish movement. He then implemented secularism and reinforced the Turkish state. It was during the Kemalist regime that religious activities were banned, Kurdish ethnicity among the Sunni Kurds was more associated with Sunni Islam and some activities like Madrasa and Tariqa on a small scale continued to function underground (Bruinessen, 1992, 36). This situation continued for a long time, until the end of the twentieth century, when again both sides started to use religion. Nevertheless, as Zubaida (1992) mentions 'even the secular Kemalist state has experienced the assertion of Islamic politics' (p. 7). The secular state practically justified the entry of the army into politics in defence of secularism, while in its invasion of Kurdistan it called for 'holy war', declaring that it is the religious duty of people to obey the state against insurgent Kurdish fighters (Bozarsalan, 1992, 112).

Secular Kurds vs. pro-Islamist Turks (1990s-)

From the 1980s the right-wing Turkish nationalism attempted to apply a Turkish-Islamic ideology as a new state ideology (Bruinessen, 1999). Like the Ba'ath ideology that made Islam an organic component of Arabism in Iraq and Syria, the Islamists developed the Turkish-Sunni Islamic Synthesis (Jongerden, 2003, 79). The Turkish regime saw purpose in using the Islamic movement and strengthened conservative Islam against the Left, especially the Kurdistan Workers' Party (PKK), founded by its leader Abdullah Öcalan (Apo) in 1978, which had attracted many Alevis (Bruinessen, 1999; Gunter, 2018, 139). In the 1980s, the PKK treated religion as a backward and reactionary force and it was active against both the state and Islamic forces (Leezenberg, 2003, 204). The regime portrayed the Marxist-Leninist rhetoric of the PKK as a danger to the Kurds' Islamic way of life (Marcus, 1993, 241). It also reinforced some Islamic groups in Kurdistan like the Islamic Liberation Army (see: White, 2000, 38) and Hezbollah (Party of God).

By developing the Kurdish question, Turkish Islamist parties, such as RP, in the 1990s criticized the state's policy and Turkey's secular tendencies for excluding and alienating the Kurds from the Turkish state, their failure in building bridges with Kurdish communities and allowing the activity of the 'secular' PKK. However, by regarding Islam as a foundation of the state and returning to the Islamic identity as an overarching umbrella and emphasizing the unity of all under Islam, the Kurds were included (Barkey and Fuller, 1998, 101; Gourlay, 2020). Their template was that of the Ottoman Empire, to regard equality for all Muslims irrespective of their ethnic background. Then, the Turkish regime used the Islamic and Ottoman heritage as a basis to conceptualize the new common national identity (Barkey and Fuller, 1998, 102; Gunes, 2012, 3). Indeed, they used this policy again to promote Turkish ethnicity. In fact, for them it was an easier way to silence and gradually assimilate the Kurds, with a simple cultural recognition, than denying their existence. The declaration of RP for Islamic solidarity appealed to the Kurds, however it underplayed the ethnic differences and was used as a tool to cover the Turkish-Kurdish division (Barkey and Fuller, 1998, 25 and 78). For example, in 1993 the leader of RP, Necmettin Erbakan, had said that "only Muslim fraternity could combat the PKK" (Türkmen, 2018). In reality, Erbakan was first and foremost a Turkish nationalist and considered the interests of Turkey and the Turkish ethno-nation above all else (Barkey and Fuller, 1998, 105). He saw the PKK as the biggest rival in Kurdistan. After capturing office as Islamist Prime Minister, on one hand he called the PKK terrorist and again talked about military intervention against the PKK, seeking Iran's assistance (White, 2000, 40). On the other hand, in 1996 he declared: "We have bonds of brotherhood. There is nothing more absurd than ethnic differentiation among Muslim brothers" (Gunter, 2011, 100). Even the Turkish armed forces had appealed to the Kurds' religious sentiments during the 1990s. Using helicopters they dropped Quranic verses such as 'Fight in the way of God against those who fight you [...] God does not like aggressive people'[10] on villages in regions where they were combatting the PKK (Gourlay, 2020). Whilst, for the Kurdish people the Turkish army

[10] The Surah of al-Baqarah (the Cow), 190.

was aggressive and like the secular Turkish regime, the PKK also described those who died in clashes as 'martyr' (Romano, 2006, 90).

The Islamists in Kurdistan strongly opposed secular ideologies especially Marxism and communism. Most notable was the Kurdish Hezbollah/KH (1980s-2000s), a militant Islamic group and a rival of PKK. The KH had Iranian connections and its leaders were under the influence of the 1979 revolution of Iran. Having an Islamic approach, Hezbollah established a considerable following amongst Kurds by articulating political Islam as a solution to the Kurdish problem. It gained popularity since Islamic sentiments were still a significant factor in Kurdish society. While some of the Hezbollah members had purely an Islamist orientation, opposed to nationalism and Alevi Kurds, others emphasized equality for the Kurds, with some in the Islamic Umma and fraternity combining Islam and nationalism to seek an Islamic Kurdish state. Nevertheless, the focus of KH on secular rivalry and targeting PKK as the Kurdistan Infidel Party[11] was welcomed by the Turkish regime to use against the PKK and other leading secular Kurdish political actors. The KH's existence, ideology and function favoured the Turkish government and was against the secular Kurdish national movement as a mainstream trend (Bruinessen, 1999; Gourlay, 2020; Gunes, 2012, 128-131; Gunter, 2018: 139). Öcalan attributed the founding of KH to the Turkish government and its Intelligence Organization acting against the Kurdish movement (Ocalan, 2018, 1066). It was "secretly encouraged by the state to protect the unity of the Muslim Turkish state the PKK was threatening to divide" (Gunter, 2011, 116). Under KH or through it, the regime assassinated a large number of PKK members and sympathizers,

---

[11] Partiye Kafirin Kurdistan

intellectuals and journalists like Musa Anter[12] (1920-1992). Indeed, it became a tool in the hands of Turkish politicians especially those from the Islamist Welfare Party (RP), and later the AKP. During the 1990s, a civil war between the PKK and KH broke out, which benefitted the Turkish government. Nevertheless, from 1995 the government lost its control over KH, then the confrontation between them began (Barkey and Fuller, 1998, 25 & 73). Afterwards, KH was removed by Turkish forces when it turned more towards Kurdishness (Elitsoy, 2017; Yavuz and Özcan, 2006). After KH, the regime alternatively founded another organization under "Kurdish Hamas" against the PKK (Ocalan, 2018, 1072). It established a new religious school and Quran classes. The ministry of religious affairs used all mosques for cultural cleansing. Religion continued to be "political and a tool to deny the entity of Kurds and to distort their struggle" (Ocalan, 2018, 1073).

By gradually revealing the intentions of Turkish politicians, however, the secular Kurds adopted a new discourse reconciled with religion to attract the religious Kurds; and the Islamist Kurds situated their religious views alongside Kurdish national demands as a reaction to the mainstream Turkish Islamist movements (Elitsoy, 2017). In this regard, the PKK incorporated some religious elements into its discourse after 1990 in reaction to the growth of the Islamic movement and political Islam in Turkey, rivalry between the pro-Kurdish people's Democracy Party (HADEP) and Welfare party, which by appealing to Islam mobilized the Kurds and increased its votes among the Sunni Kurds, as well as the secularist propaganda of Kemalist nationalists and politicians to attract the Alevis, and contestation between the PKK and the KH for Kurdish leadership in 80s and 90s. The PKK, while still Marxist-Leninist, moved away from blaming Islam and began to respect religion as an important

---

[12] Apê Musa

social force and acknowledged its role in Kurdish society in order to bolster its own appeal to observant Kurds, but emphasized more on ethno-national rights (Gunes, 2012, 128; Leezenberg, 2003, 204; Marcus, 1993, 242). Accordingly, in contrast to anti-Kurdish Islamists, Ocalan finally presented a new analysis of the history and role of religion, especially Islam, in society. Criticizing religious history and Islam, and even seeking to reform it (see: Ocalan, 2006), he indeed censured the use of religion by current states too.[13] Against the religious propaganda of the Turkish state to remove the name Kurdistan, he sanctified Kurdistan as the land of prophets (see: ibid.). Ocalan emphasized the role of concepts like freedom, equality and justice in Islam to legitimate the Kurdish movement (Gunes, 2012, 129).

Thus, the PKK gradually adopted a more and more populist ideology and moved towards multiculturalism to include Sunni Islam, Alevism and Êzidîtî/Izidism to mobilize the Kurdish people. It took a pragmatic approach to the political function of religion, creating representative organizations among religious communities in Kurdistan and used some religious concepts and positive aspects of religion (Gunes, 2012, 110; Leezenberg, 2003, 204). It fostered pro-PKK religious tendencies, and softened its attitude towards Kurdish Sunni Islamists. The PKK then founded organizations such as the pro-PKK Islamic Movement of Kurdistan (Hereketa Islamiya Kurdistane), which emerged in

---

[13] Ocalan believes that if religion to be defined only materialistically, it will be very dangerous. The role of religion in society and its institutes should be understood (Ocalan, 2002, 131). He prominently considers Islam and its revolutionary importance in the evolutionary process of civilization (see: Ocalan, 2018, 1004). He tries to analyze the realities expressed by Islam and introduces Islam as 'the revolutionary force of the feudal era' (Ocalan, 2002, 128). Ocalan describes the advent of Islam as the biggest revolution in history (Gunes, 2012, 129) and Prophet Muhammad as a revolutionary personality for all historical periods (Ocalan, 2002, 135). He criticizes state Islam within which the state abuses Islam ideologically, legally and economically. For him state religion is not a real religion and has lost its religious nature (Ocalan, 2018, 1010). Conversely, he tries to liken his path to the path of prophets so that he says "the first migration was the one I followed in the path of Prophet Abraham towards Syria and Lebanon…" (ibid., 1049) and "After a two month journey, like the journey of Prophet Abraham, I found myself among Palestinians…" (ibid., 1179).

1993 through links with Sunni clerics, Union of Religious Persons and the Union of Patriotic Imams. In 1995, criticizing the KH, Öcalan "declared PKK to be the real fighter for Islam understood as a religion of justice against all kinds of oppression" (Türkmen, 2018). The PKK also accommodated itself to other communities to attract them. It founded and fostered affiliated religious associations like the Kurdish Alevi and Êzîdî Unions (Barkey and Fuller, 1998, 25 & 70; Bruinessen, 1999; White, 2000, 48). Against the influence of PKK among Alevi Kurds, the regime also developed Alevism as an alternative to Kurdish identity and nationalism. Nevertheless, the conflict between Alevis and Sunnis affected the Sunni-led government's plan and made many Alevi Kurds closer to the PKK as a secular party (see: Bruinessen, 1996).

Turkish state's use of Sunni-Alevi cleavage in Bakûr

As mentioned, Alevis historically supported the Republican People's Party, founded by Ataturk, because of the party's claim to secularism, as well as their fear of re-establishing a Sunni Islamic state. Among the Alevi Kurds[14], their religious identity was more dominant until the last decades of the twentieth century because of the state's policies that declared them as Turks and regarded them as supporters of secularism (Chelik, 2003, 143), as well as belonging to a religious minority. Moreover, attempts by Islamists at the Sunnification of Turkey from the 1970s led to manifestations of Alevi identity on a political plane. When the state in the 1980s and 1990s moved towards Sunni identity, tolerating Islamic fundamentalism despite its secularist claim, almost like in time of Ataturk again the Alevi Turks tended towards Kemalists and Alevi Kurds towards Leftists, especially the PKK considering the emergence of Islamists, Islamic danger,

---

[14] About two-thirds of all Alevis in Turkey are currently Turk, some of whom were originally Kurdish and were linguistically and ethnically assimilated. Moreover, some Alevis were also gradually religiously assimilated into the Sunnis (Chelik, 2003, 142 & 150).

a Sunni Islamic state and the return to an Ottoman-period situation (Kehl-Bodrogi, 2003, 67). Islamists under the Islamic Welfare Party gained support among the majority of Sunni Muslims including the Kurds. In contrast to the Welfare Party, the Kemalist nationalists tried to use the emergence of Islamism to attract Alevis. They introduced political Islam as the most serious threat and convinced many Alevis to maintain their allegiance to the secular state. In this regard, the 'Alevi Manifesto', including their demand for official recognition and equal rights, was published in the Cumhuriyet/Jumhuriyat daily in 1990 (Leezenberg, 2003, 200 & 209). Government officials like Suleyman Demirl and Mesut Yilmaz participated in an Alevi festival. In particular, they tried to convert Alevi Kurds and insisted that originally they were Turks (Jongerden, 2003, 82).

However, by tending towards the Kurdish national movement and PKK among the Alevi Kurds, the state tried to use Alevism along with Islamism against the Kurdish movement (Jongerden, 2003, 72; Vorhoff, 2003, 96). In the 1970s and 1980s deadly confrontations between Sunnis and Alevis in some parts of Kurdistan led to the rise of Alevi sentiments more than their Kurdish nationalist attitudes. In the 1980s, in order to prevent Alevi Kurds' support for the PKK, the Turkish state's policies supported these growing sentiments and Alevi Identity, which for the Turkish state was less of a danger than Kurdish identity. It granted a certain formal recognition by allowing public ceremonies and publications. Nevertheless, in the 1990s the government's move towards Sunni-Islamists increased Alevi sympathies for the PKK (Chelik, 2003, 148-152). In contrast to the Kemalists, Ocalan attributed the increase of sectarian activities such as the political and cultural activity by Alevis in Kurdistan to the MIT (Turkish political police) who wanted to stop the development of Kurdish national consciousness and feeling. Reinvigorating their movement among Alevi Kurds, in

1994 the PKK created the Alevi Kurdish Federation and published a magazine for them called Zulfaqar (the name of Imam Ali's sword) and painted headbands with the portrait of Seyid Reza (Leezenberg, 2003, 204-5; White, 2000, 49). It tried to use the symbols and characters of Alevis, such as Ali and Husain, to portray Alevis as the oppressed against the state as a symbol of tyranny (Jongerden, 2003, 82).

Electoral function of religion in Bakûr

During the rule of the Kemalists, apart from a latent function in maintaining the integrity of the state's territory due to the Sunni majority, religion was at least used in elections because a significant majority of people had retained Islamic identity and adherence. From the 1950s the major secular parties have used religious sentiments to secure votes through the influence of sheikhs in Kurdistan. For example, in the 1950s, against the government and its secular disposition, the Democratic Party of Turkey used the remaining Sufi networks of south-eastern Anatolia to gain Kurdish votes (Gourlay, 2020). Via sheikhs it persuaded their followers that a vote for the party meant religious freedom (White, 2000, 34). From the 1970s and especially the 1980s, Right-wing religious parties like RP and then AKP have had a Kurdish constituency (Zubaida, 1992, 7). The Kurdish vote was vital to these parties to become a majority party. Benefitting from the Islamic nature of the society, RP created a link with Kurdish society through the religious orders which are prevalent among the Kurds. Since it appeared as an opposition, on one hand, and the legal pro-Kurdish parties such as the People's labor Party (HEP) founded in 1990 and its successors were not strong yet, on the other, the RP attracted the support of Kurds and Kurdish votes in the 1994 municipal elections and became a serious contender for the Kurdish vote in the 1995 parliament elections. Some of the Kurdish nationalist activists also saw an opportunity in the RP and its successors to democratize the political system and push it further. Nevertheless, when the RP adopted the state's discourse it disappointed its own Kurdish activists (Barkey and Fuller, 1998, 79 & 103-106).

AKP was another Islamic party that used an Islamist cooptation aimed at soothing Kurdish demands. By using Islamism, it introduced itself as against Kemalist ideology. It identified secularism as a cause of division between Turks and Kurds and offered Islam and Islamic brotherhood as a solution to ethnic tensions and long-running Kurdish grievances, as well as a means to bridge ethnic divisions on the basis that the majority of both Kurds and Turks are Sunni Muslims (Gourlay, 2020). It divided Kurdistan between Islamic and non-Islamic identities and has used the cleavage in elections since 2002. By pronouncing the PKK and the pro-Kurdish parties as anti-religious organizations in its public religious activities, and using religious groups like the descendants of KH (organizations like Mustazaf-Der, a Kurdish Islamic organization based in Diyarbakır), Naqshbandi and Nurcu networks, AKP received a sizable vote in the Kurdish regions (Bahcheli and Noel, 2010; Yahuz and Ozcan, 2006). The religious aspect of Islamic organizations was often used against the Kurdish movement. For example, in the general election of 2007, Mustazaf-Der asked its community to vote for the AKP candidates rather than the secularist candidates of the Democratic Society Party (DTP), founded in 2005 (Elitsoy, 2017). Consequently, AKP support was boosted in Kurdistan. It showed a strong performance in the election amongst Kurdish voters, and outpolled the main pro-Kurdish party. In six Kurdish-populated provinces the AKP claimed a winning 44 percent of the vote compared with the main pro-Kurdish party's 38 percent (Gourlay, 2020).

Following the emergence of the AKP as an electoral threat when the Kurdish actors lost the Kurdish votes to it, the Kurdish political movement tried to reappraise its relationship with Islam to reclaim political territory from the AKP. The DTP, connecting Imams, designated a place for Islamic leaders amongst its delegates. The DTP, then HDP (Peoples' Democratic Party) founded in 2012, sought to incorporate Islamic sensibilities into their political offering in order to appeal to Kurdish constituents (ibid.). On the other hand, apart from the nationalistic stance of the Islamic Party of Kurdistan (PÎK)[15], a Kurdish nationalist and Islamist party (Bruinessen, 2000; White, 2000, 38) that also supported HDP, the descendants of KH had more Kurdishness. They mostly affiliated with a wing of KH which had developed a form of Islamism accommodating Kurdish nationalism (Bruinessen, 1999). For example, although for the Free Cause Party[16], founded in 2012, based on the Quran, Hadith, and sayings of the Prophet Muhammad, ethnic nationalism was incompatible with the Umma, they emphasized an Islamic approach to solve the discriminatory injustice against the Kurds (Elitsoy, 2017).

Through changes in AKP policy against the Kurds, gradually most of the Kurdish religio-ethnic elites understood that the AKP government interpreted religious teachings in favour of its politics. Consequently, the Kurdish political movement asserted a distinct Islam in the lead up to the 2011 general election. Selahattin Demirtaş and Gültan Kışanak, co-chairs of the Peace and Democracy Party (BDP),[17] played upon Islamic sensibilities in their rhetoric, demanding Kurdish sermons to be given in mosques. Moreover, religiously inclined Kurds, pointing to the Quranic verse about human diversity, emphasized a distinctive Kurdish identity and dismissed the AKP's idea of 'Islamic brotherhood' primarily as assimilationist. Similarly, the Kurdish

---

[15] Partiya Îslamiya Kurdistan
[16] Partiya Doza Azadî (Huda-Par)
[17] BDP succeeded DTP in 2008 and succeeded by HDP in 2014.

religious actors, such as the members of KH, who previously upheld a purely Islamic identity, increasingly emphasized a Kurdish identity within an Islamic context. In the same year, a leading figure in Mustazaf-Der using an Islamic perspective defended Kurdish rights. Arguing the acceptance of ethnic and linguistic diversity by Islam, he asked for freedom for the Kurdish language, education in Kurdish, and celebration of Kurdish culture (Gourlay, 2020). Melas (religious figures) in Kurdistan reacted to the restrictions on the Kurdish language in 2011-2013. As civilian disobedience, they held prayers in outdoor locations, boycotting 'official' mosques seen to be instruments of state control in Kurdish-populated cities. They read their own sermons in Kurdish, with pro-Kurdish ethno-nationalist messages focusing on Quranic verses related to Kurdish identity instead of the Turkish sermons dictated by the state's highest religious authority - the Presidency of Religious Affairs or the Diyanet. Because of his fear of losing widespread support among Kurdish voters, Recep Tayyip Erdoğan voiced his disapproval of these gatherings. In retaliation, BDP deputy Sebahat Tuncel called for an end to the monopolization of beliefs. Thus, the Kurdish political parties performed more strongly in 2011, and in subsequent elections (Gourlay, 2020; Türkmen, 2018).

In line with the AKP's Islamist programme, in December 2011, the Diyanet declared its intention to hire 1000 Kurdish Melas as state-employed Imams. This was for political purposes so that in February 2012, the government decided to give the Diyanet a more active role in the fight against terrorism (Türkmen, 2018). Conversely, Öcalan called for a 'Democratic Islam Congress' in Diyarbakır in 2013. He cited examples of the Prophet Mohammad conducting Shura (councils) as a means of consultation and decision making. He portrayed the congress as a way of working against 'groups betraying Islam' (ibid.). Nevertheless, AKP continued its religio-political attempts in

Kurdistan. In the electoral campaign of June 2015, Erdoğan appealed to religion and attempted to sway Kurdish voters by calling upon their Islamic impulses. He declared the HDP anti-Islam. While brandishing a Kurdish-language Quran, he told an audience, the HDP has 'nothing to do with Islam' (Gourlay, 2020). He labeled HDP leader Selahattin Demirtaş as a Zoroastrian.[18]

In general, concerning the Kurdish issue the Islamist parties in Turkey such as RP, Fazilet/Virtue Party (FP) and AKP have not been "less nationalist than the secular parties" (Bahcheli and Noel, 2010). Although, as Türkmen (2018) mentions, Islam can be seen as a factor for peace, conciliation and solving Turkish/Kurdish conflict in Turkey because of its social role and political effect as a common religion in society. Nevertheless, the Turkish political actors put forward Islam as a means to assimilate Kurds in Northern Kurdistan. In reaction, the Kurdish actors utilize Islam to legitimate their stance on Kurdish rights (Gourlay, 2020). Such a situation is also seen in the other three countries.

---

[18] Noah Blaser, "Who represents Turkey's Kurds?" Available, Jan 2021, at: http://platform24. org/en/articles/289/who-represents-

IRAQ: ARAB-KURDISH CONFRONTATION IN BAŞÛR

Kurdish revolt against the non-Muslim pro-Arab British Mandate (1921-1932)

The Ottoman Empire was occupied by the Allies at the end of WWI. It resulted in detaching and forming new countries including Iraq and Syria based on the Sykes-Picot agreement (1916) between France and Britain. Iraq was created by the British in 1921. By October 1921 Churchill accepted that 'Kurds are not to be under Arabs if they do not wish' (Fieldhouse, 2001, 38). During the colonial rule and prior to the formal annexation to Iraq in 1925-26, Başûr was dealt with by the colonial powers as a separate political and administrative entity (Aziz and Kirmanj, 2018; Rafaat, 2018, 52). Nevertheless, contrary to the 1920 Treaty of Sevres, Başûr was formally annexed. Iraqi Arab nationalism that had initially started 'as a reaction to Young Turk policies, developed under the British occupation' (Maóz, 1999, 13) and became the dominant nationalism, while the Kurdish national movement continued to struggle for political rights. Against the Kurdish movement, the dominant Sunni government and politicians appealed to the old tool, i.e. common religion, here the Sunni sect, between the majority of Kurds and Sunni Arabs to attract, integrate and assimilate Kurds and neutralize Kurdish nationalism.

The Kurdish independence movement started in 1918, before the creation of the Iraqi state, under the leadership of

51

Sheikh Mahmoud Barzinji (1878-1956)[1], an influential religious chief, who was the leader of a series of Kurdish uprisings until 1932 (Aziz and Kirmanj, 2018; Rafaat, 2018, 52). Demanding an independent Kurdish state, he revolted against British rule in Iraq. Sheikh Mahmoud founded his first government in October 1918. With the beginning of Turkish propaganda under Islam and Kurdish unrest in early 1919, he began secret dealings with the Turks (Gunter, 2011, 12). Although the British government was trying to work out some form of indirect rule through him, nevertheless by imprisoning some British officers he declared his independence (Fieldhouse, 2001, 69 & 99). Indeed, the Sheikh's first revolt was affected by the religious propaganda of Kemalist Turks and he provoked by them so that he allied himself with Ataturk's forces like the majority of Sunni Kurds in Bakûr (Romano, 2006, 186). It led to a disagreement between the Sheikh and Britain and the British suppressed his revolt by military force in June 1919 (Olson, 1989, 53). Afterwards, against the Turks, a joint Iraqi-British declaration recognized the Kurds' political right within the Iraqi frontier in 1922. In that year, the second Kurdish government was formed and Sheikh Mahmoud became "the king of Kurdistan" (1922-1924). Thus, the British recognized the authority of the Sheikh as ruler and referred to the autonomous entity as the 'Kurdish state'. [2]

Nevertheless, Sheikh Mahmoud was still under the influence of the Turks' politics and the religious connection with them, as well as the religious conflict with the non-Muslim British. He was also alleged to have negotiated with the Turks for an independent Kurdistan under his leadership in 1923. Moreover, against King Faisal (1883-1933) who used his race as Hashemi Arab to gain legitimacy, the Sheikh as a religious figure had a remarkable

---

[1] He was from family of Barzinja Sheikhs and son of Sheikh Said who, as mentioned, had been killed in 1909.
[2] Accordingly, British officials and scholars commonly used the term 'Southern Kurdistan' until the mid-1940s (Rafaat, 2018, 52).

traditional influence in Kurdish society. They were rivals at the spearhead of Arab and Kurdish independence. However, the disputes between Iraqi and Kurdish governments led to an attack by the Iraqi government, and subsequently war broke out between the two parties in 1923-24. Eventually, the Sheikh was again suppressed by British forces. The Iraqi government under British mandate even used Christian Assyrians in its army against the Sheikh.[3] Instead of a regiment of Muslim cavalry, the Assyrian troops were used to occupy Silêmanî. Then, the Iraqi Sunni rulers started using religion in common with the Kurds. For example, the King of Iraq in 1924 visited Hewlêr. While he was not a religious person, he used the religious personality of the well-known and influential Mela, Abubakir Afendi, and ritual of the Friday Prayer to affect people (see: Fieldhouse, 2001, 46 & 141-164). Despite this, the Kurds intermittently enjoyed a degree of self-rule for several years, until after further revolts, eventually in 1932 the Sheikh's revolts and the British mandate ended.

Arab-Kurdish religious politics in Independent Iraq (1932-)

After Sheikh Mahmoud, the Kurdish movement continued under the leadership of Mela Mustafa Barzani. His power was grounded on his family's religious authority as Naqshbandi sheikhs. Mela Mustafa's charismatic personality prevented Iraqi public figures from having any impact on ordinary Kurds. His family had many religious supporters, especially his brother Sheikh Ahmad Barzani, who was an important clerical leader of Kurdistan. However, in 1932–33 the revolt of Sheikh Ahmad and

---

[3] At the time, due to Muslim sentiments against the Allies as non-Muslim occupiers of the Islamic Caliphate during WWI, as well as the lack of mutual trust, the Allies usually used the religious minorities. The common religion between the British forces and Assyrians paved the way for their further cooperation. Such cooperation had already taken place in Rojhelat so that the Allies' support to Assyrians paved the way for conflict between Shikaks, under Simko, and Assyrians in 1918-1922 in favour of Qajar rule. In Başûr the British also had a similar policy (See: Fieldhouse, 2001, 154).

Mela Mustafa was suppressed (Fieldhouse, 2001, 42; Gunter, 2011, 13; Rafaat, 2018, 81; Romano, 2006, 188). Iraqi rulers continued their Sunnist politics to unite Sunni Arabs and Kurds against the Shia majority who didn't support the government and were alienated by the brutal suppression of a rising in the Euphrates region in 1935–36 (Fieldhouse, 2001, 32). Nevertheless, Mustafa Barzani incited another major uprising in 1943. Although the third stage of the Kurdish movement had already started under the leadership of political parties, the Kurdish secular nationalists used Barzani's influence as their leader. The continuity of the Kurdish revolt led to the recognition of Kurdish autonomy in Başûr in 1970, which came to an end when disputes developed between the Iraqi regime and the Kurdish leadership in 1974; and the Kurdish movement was again suppressed in 1975.

After the death of Barzani in 1979 and from the middle of the 1980s, along with the mainstream secular nationalist movement under the leadership of the Kurdistan Democratic Party (PDK) founded in 1946 and the Patriotic Union of Kurdistan (PUK) founded in 1975, the Islamic Movement of Kurdistan also emerged. It too had nationalist demands, though within the framework of Islamic ideology. The Islamic movement associated with the Iranian regime to secure its help against the Ba'ath regime, but it became a tool in the hands of the Iranian and then the Iraqi government. These governments exploited the secular-religious gap among the Kurds against the Kurdish nationalist movement, and succeeded in dividing the Kurdish movement which led to civil wars in the following decade (for more details see: Mofidi, 2015c). In this period, moreover, other small religious parties affiliated to the main secular parties emerged, like "Kurdish Hezbollah" under the leadership of Sheikh Muhammad Khalid Barzani in the 1980s (Bruinessen, 1992, 40). Thus, the secular parties also tried to use the social influence of religion and the support of Iran's Islamic regime against the Iraqi regime, while Iran needed them as Islamic parties under the control of Tehran to fight against its enemy, the Ba'ath regime (See: Bruinessen, 2000).

On the other hand, the secular governments of Iraq used Islamization to Arabize Kurdistan; during the Ba'ath regime by demonizing the Kurdish Zagrossian civilization in Iraqi textbooks, and later by ignoring the existence of such a civilization. "The Iraqi textbooks glorify Islamic conquests and the process of Arabisation and Islamisation of the conquered people" (Rafaat, 2018, 37). The Ba'athists used religious trends in Kurdistan to influence the ordinary Kurdish people, with some officials connected with Kurdish trends and figures. For example, Izzat Ibrahim al-Douri, Saddam's deputy, had a close relationship with the family of Kesnezani/Kasnazani Sheikhs, a branch of the Qadiriyya order which wielded a broad influence in society, some members of this family having important positions in the regime.

The Nationalist Ba'athists, using nerve gas and chemical weapons perpetrated a massacre, destroying towns and relocating many Kurds in Kurdistan (see: Aziz and Kirmanj, 2018; Rafaat, 2018, 45). While being secular, they justified their actions by religion (Bruinessen, 1992, 43). For example, 'Al-Anfal' an Arabic-Quranic word meaning 'spoils of battle'[4] was used by the Ba'athists as the code name for a series of their operations against the Kurds. 'Anfal operations' in 1988, known as the Kurdish Genocide, had a devastating impact on Kurdistan and resulted in the killing of thousands of civilian inhabitants (Karadaghi, 1993, 225; Kirmanj and Rafaat, 2020). In the same year, on March 16, Halabja had its turn, when a chemical attack on the town left at least five thousand dead (Farrokh, 2011, 404; Romano, 2006,

[4] It is the name of a chapter/Surah of the Quran, where the rules of war and rights of conquest were allegedly revealed to the Prophet Muhammad after the battle of Badr in 624 AD.

199-200). They carried out the Anfal campaign, despite the fact that in the Arab-Kurd dispute the problem was not a religious issue and the Kurds were not infidels to be killed and their estate taken. According to Rafaat (2018, 140) Iraqi behaviour in the Anfal was affected by the de-Kurdification policy.

Since the 1990s, and especially after the collapse of the Ba'ath regime in 2003, the Kurds were given an autonomous status within the federal state of Iraq. Even so, the dominant Shiite government in Iraq under the influence of the Iranian Shiite regime stood against Kurdish nationalism. It used the political, economic and military support of Iran as a Shiite state to solidify the Shiite Arab government. At the same time, the religious link between the majority of Kurds as Sunni and the central government was cut off. The government tried to reinforce the Shiite minority in Kurdistan and developed religious rituals among them, including some of the Seyyid families.[5] Moreover, it reconnected with branches of religious orders. Conversely, the Kurds tried to take advantage of the religious cleavage among Arabs and were more inclined to support the Sunni Arabs against the central government. Apart from an unofficial referendum launched in 2005 which was not officially supported by the KRG or Kurdish political parties (Rafaat, 2018, 197), on September 25, 2017 in an official referendum 93 percent of Kurds voted for independence. Nevertheless, the Iraqi government attacked Kurdistan and did not permit it to proclaim its independence. Tehran, Baghdad and Ankara cooperated against Başûr. Iran openly declared its disapproval (Aziz and Kirmanj, 2018; Akbarzadeh et al. 2019). It backed the Iraqi government creating a political sphere against the Kurds during the referendum and then sent in its troops to

---

[5] For example, with the participation of Shiite personalities, the Seyyids of Barzinja in Silêmanî held the mourning rites of Ashura in 2019 (See a report about their ritual on 9/9/2019, available, 7/9/2021, at: https://www.rudaw.net/sorani/kurdistan/ 090920199). Also, the rites were held in Kesnezanî Tekiye in August 2021.

help the Iraqi Shi'i militia in their attack on Kurdistan, especially the city of Kirkuk (Mohammadpour and Soleimani, 2020).

SYRIA: ARAB-KURDISH CONFRONTATION IN ROJAVA

The impact of Islamic discourse during French Mandate (1921-1946)

After the collapse of the Ottoman Empire, Syria was another detached country. In Syria, under French colonial rule (1921-1946), Arab-Kurdish relations were fairly good (Nazdar, 1993, 198). The actors in the Kurdish cultural movement found collaborators in the mandatory administration. In the 1920s, various communities followed a parallel evolution. Nevertheless, the Arabs gradually used ethno-national fervour and religious sentiments against the pluralist policy of France, which led to their dominance. At the beginning, the conflict between the Turks and the Allies reinforced the Arab nationalists. As it had against the British in Iraq, the Turkish state tried to use Islamic propaganda and the Muslim brotherhood to turn the Arabs and Kurds against France in Syria during the 1920s-1930s (Tejel, 2009, 12, 23 & 32). Moreover, the religious connection between the majority of Kurds and Arabs as Sunni, on the one hand, and the diversity of religions including Êzîdî/Izidi, Christian, and Jews in Rojava, on the other, influenced unity of the Kurds in favour of Arab nationalism (Fuccaro, 2003, 196).

Along with the growth of Arab nationalist demands, from 1924 onwards the Kurds demanded autonomy for themselves and submitted their petitions. With the appearance of Arab nationalist organizations such as the People's Party, established in 1925, and the Syrian Union Party (see: Khoury, 1987, 144-147), the Kurdish nationalists under the leaders of the Khoyboun/Xwebûn League[1], with the help of influential Sheikhs and the Melas such as Sheikh 'Abd al-Rahman Garisi, an active member of the Khoyboun, tried to nationalize Kurdish ethnic identity especially through Quranic schools from 1927. In 1928 they submitted a memorandum oriented towards local autonomy, demanding the replacement of all functionaries in the Kurdish regions by Kurds; teaching in the Kurdish language for Kurds; and the constitution of a Kurdish regiment to guard the northern frontier, probably against the Turks invasion on Kurds (Tejel, 2009, 27-28 & 96).

In the following decade, more Syrian Arab nationalist organizations[2] appeared with some of them, such as the National Bloc, gaining power, while they all tried to achieve independence. Although these parties were secular, they took advantage of religious issues. The Arabs exploited the arrival of Assyrian refugees in Jazira in 1933 and the requests of numerous Jews wanting to settle in Syria. They propagated that France had a Zionist project similar to that in Palestine to tap into religious sentiments against France. Thus, this affected the Kurds. Although the formation of the autonomist Kurdo-Christian bloc in 1936 influenced and slightly changed the discourse, by signing the Franco-Syrian Treaty, which foreshadowed the independence of Syria, the Franco-Kurdish collaboration ended in 1936 (ibid., 29-33).

With uprisings against the colonial rule, moreover, Syrian nationalists like Abd al-Rahman Shahbandar (1879-1940), who was

---

[1] A Kurdish nationalist organization founded in Lebanon in 1927 and active in Bakûr and Rojava, which then led in 1930 to the Ararat uprising in Bakûr.
[2] The National Bloc founded in 1929 (formally 1932), the Syrian National Party founded in 1932, the Syrian Social Nationalist Party founded in 1932, League of National Action established in 1933, United National Front established in 1935-8, the National Youth Party founded in 1939 (which became the Arab Socialist Party in 1950 and then was merged with the Ba'ath Party in 1953).

supported by Islamic leaders such as Wahid al-Hakim and Mustafa al-Zarqa, launched a pan-Islamic campaign in 1937 that affected the Kurdish people and attracted the Kurdish religious elites (Fuccaro, 2003, 213). They used Islamic sentiments and raised Islamic discourse including Islamic terms and symbols, especially 'holy war', against infidels in their uprisings. Meanwhile, the Kurdish nationalists continued their strife for an autonomist movement. It was important in 1938. Their alliance with the Christians, which was supported by their religious leaders, broadened their influence. The Arab nationalists opposed the autonomist movement of Kurds and Christians (Tejel, 2009, 16, 30-34).

Although the Kurds made progress in achieving some of their demands between 1928 and 1936, thus, under the pressure of Arab nationalists in the 1930s, official politics no longer supported local autonomies and ethnic minorities. Because of the Arabs' opposition to Kurdish education, the Kurds inevitably adopted diverse strategies to preserve their language such as teaching Kurdish in the Quranic schools which simultaneously acted as "Kurdish schools", night classes, and various individual efforts. Kurdish was the primary language of communication in the religious schools in Rojava in the 1930s-1940s (ibid., 26, 29 & 97).

In the early 1940s the unionist Arab nationalists in the name of Muslim brotherhood between Arabs and Kurds provoked their Muslim neighbours against Christians and used Islamic ideology to weaken Kurdish nationalism. Thus, they damaged the autonomist Kurdish–Christian bloc (ibid., 36). Moreover, the secular and even non-Muslim Arab nationalists such as Constantin K. Zurayk (1909-2000), a liberal, and Michel Aflagh (1910-89)[3], both Christian, used Islam and regarded it as part of

---

[3] One of the leaders of Arab Ba'ath (i.e. Resurrection or Renaissance) Movement from 1940-1, as well as one of the founders of the Arab Socialist Ba'ath Party, founded in Damascus initially in

Arabic nationalism. For them Islam was the inspiration of the Arab nation and where there was Islam, there was Arabism (See: Kedourie, 1992, 298; Mofidi, 2015a, 48). Finally, although Kurdish deputies again in 1945 presented their demands to the president of the Republic, Shukri al-Quwatli[4], and despite the government's promises, the mandate period ended in 1946 without Kurdish demands being met. Tied to Sunni Islam, now, the Arab nationalists were fully dominant in independent Syria (Tejel, 2009, 37-9).

Using Islam against Kurds by the secular Arab state (1946-)

Despite being a secular state since the independence of Syria in 1946, the government has used Islam as an assimilating tool against Kurds, as well as a base for nonsectarian Alawi-Sunni alliance in favour of Arab nationalism as one of the main components of the Syrian regime's national integration policy (see: Maóz, 1999, xiii & 68), especially during the Assad family's power until the 2000s. After independence, there were two trends among Syrian political actors; the followers of Syrian national identity, and Arab nationalism. Arab nationalism in a mixed format of pan-Arabism and Arab socialism, gradually became the dominant identity (Schøtt, 2017). Non-Arab identity was not tolerated. Although two of the first five Syrian rulers[5] were originally Kurds who had a secular and neutral strategy, both secular and religious Arab nationalist organizations such as the National Party (1947-1963), the People's Party (1948-1963), the Muslim Brotherhood of Syria founded in 1945[6] and the Ba'ath,

---

1943 and formally in 1947.

[4] From the National Bloc until 1947 and then National Party.

[5] Husni al-Za'im in 1949 (his prime minister, Muhsin al-Barazi, was also of some Kurdish descent) and Adib al-Shishakli in 1953-54.

[6] Its activities began as Islamic Jam'iyyat (Muslim Association) in the 1930s. After independence, the conflict between the Muslim Brotherhood and the army began, especially with the coup of Husni al-Zaim and then Adib al-Shishakli.

stood up against them and ended even the nominal presence of Kurds in the system (Tejel, 2009, 40-45). The formation of a homogeneous Arab-Muslim state started and the use of languages other than Arabic was restricted (Yildiz, 2005, 31). At the end of the 1950s Arab Nationalists fully dominated and stopped all Kurdish activities (see: Tejel, 2009, 48). In contrast, the Kurdish movement especially under parties like the Kurdish Democratic Party in Syria (KDP-S)[7] founded in 1957, continued (see: Vanly, 1968, 7).

Arab political leaders used Islamic discourse and institutions against the Kurdish leaders, while both parties were secular. On the one hand, the Kurdish question was severely affected by the Palestine question at that time, and by justifying their nationalism with Islamism the Arab leaders attributed the Kurdish nationalism to Zionism (Yildiz, 2005, 31). On the other hand, they tried to centralize religious institutions to use and control religious activities by their favourite religious leaders. By creating the Ministry of Waqf in 1961, the regime used the centralized structure of the Sunni religious establishment to exert more control over it than in the previous period between 1949 and 1961, when the religious leaders were free to manoeuvre their way up. In the next government, the establishment became a tool in the hands of Arab nationalists against Kurds. With the end of the conservative regime in 1963, pan-Arabist Ba'athists came into

---

[7] Apart from KDPS or "The Party" (Partiya Demokrat a Kurdî li Suriyê), the Kurdish movement in Syria has included many other Kurdish political parties like: Kurdish Democratic Union Party in Syria (Partiya Yekîtî ya Demokrat a Kurdî li Suriyê), Kurdish Democratic Progressive Party in Syria (Partiya Demokrat a Pêshverû ya Kurdî li Suriyê), Kurdish Union Party in Syria (Partiya Yekitî ya Kurdî li Suriyê), Kurdih Freedom Party in Syria (Partiya Azadî ya Kurd li Sûriyê), Kurdish Democratic Party in Syria (Partiya Demokrat a Kurdî li Suriyê), Partiya Çep a Kurdî li Suriyê (Kurdish Left Party in Syria), Kurdish Democratic Progressive Party in Syria (Partiya Demokrat a Pêshverû ya Kurdî li Suriyê), Kurdish Democratic Patriotic Party in Syria (Partiya Demokrat a Welatparêz a Kurdî li Suriyê), The Syrian Kurdish Democratic Party (Partiya Demokrat a Kurdî ya Surî), Democratic Union Party (Partiya Yekîtiya Demokrat), Syrian Kurdish Democratic Concord Party (Rêkeftina Demokrat a Kurdî ya Surî), Kurdish Future Movement in Syria (Shepêla Pêsherojê ya Kurdî li Suriyê) (See: Tejel, 2009, 139).

power. In 1964 they used the Ministry of Waqf in the election of an originally Kurdish Sheikh, Ahmad Kuftaru (1915-2004), to the post of Grand Mufti of the Syrian Republic to implement their policies (Tejel, 2009, 53 & 97). Thus, Islam and Muslim brotherhood were used to cover ethno-national cleavages, as well as the Kurdish nationalistic demands.

In the 1960s teaching Kurdish language was forbidden and the Ba'ath party launched a plan to Arabize parts of Kurdish areas. For instance, on November 12, 1963 an Arab nationalist and former chief of the Secret Security Services in Hasaka, Lieutenant Muhamed Talab al-Hilal, published a security report on Kurds which proposed a twelve-point plan including the solution for and a guide to managing the Kurdish issue, as well as the necessary measures to eliminate the "Kurdish danger" in Syria. Two of the points were related to using religion. He made the state aware of the influence of Kurdish Ulama who did not "speak an acceptable form of Arabic." The sixth point of the report recommended: "the deportation of Kurdish religious Ulama (clerics) to the south who would be replaced by Arab Ulama." The seventh point about "the implementation of a 'divide-and-rule' policy against the Kurds" might be related to reinforcement of conflicts between religious minorities in Kurdistan including Muslims, Christians, Êzîdîs etc. which could be part of it. In line with Hilal's plan, in 1965 the Ba'ath leadership started to make an "Arab belt" along the Turkish border where the citizenship of many Kurdish people was revoked in Jazira (Nazdar, 1993, 200; Schøtt, 2017; Tejel, 2009, 7 & 60-61; Vanly, 1992, 155-7; Yildiz, 2005, 34).[8]

After 1966, because of the political influence of Hafez al-Assad, an Alawite, as Minister of Defence and then the leader of Syria, the Ba'athist regime became dominated by Alawites. The

---

[8] For more information about the genocide of Kurds in Syria, see: Vanly, 1968.

dominance of Shiite Alawites over the Sunnis even in the economy was evident (Kedourie, 1992, 304 & 334). At the end of the 1960s there were functional alliances between Alawites, as a religious minority, and Kurds. Hafez al-Assad used his Alawite and Kurdish networks to gain power (Tejel, 2009, 62). Nevertheless, considering the strategic strength of the Arabic Alawi-Sunni alliance, Assad saw the Kurds as a threat to his Arabic state and kept a distance from Kurdish political forces. Instead, he appealed to foreign supporters, especially in the Shiite Perso-Iranian state with which he had religious connections, and also where the Kurdish question was a common danger for both states. Thus, gradually Alawites became more dominant.

This Alawite domination gradually led to a conflict between the Sunni majority and the Alawite minority; however, by gaining power Assad understood the importance of the Sunni Arabs to keep his power and continued a pan-Arabism policy. In the 1970s, although a few Kurds held office, provided that they did not show any particular Kurdish identity, Assad brought strong measures to bear in his dealings with the Kurds, especially KDP-S (ibid., 66). He also continued to create an Arab belt between the Kurds of Rojava and those of Bakûr and Başûr in Turkey and Iraq (Gunter, 2011, 135). From 1975 the Syrian Ba'ath regime decided to rewrite Arab history. Under Arabism, it emphasized unity at all times and politically and culturally unifying trends. Some of the Kurdish "heroes," such as Salah al-Din Ayyubi[9], had been elevated to the level of a national symbol, without any mention of their ethnic origins. To implement the policy, the regime used the obvious Muslim identity of the majority of the Kurds, which is also common to the majority of Arabs (Tejel, 2009, 64).

During the Muslim Brotherhood's revolt in Hama against

---

[9] The leader and founder of the Kurdish Ayyubid state in Syria and Egypt in 12th century.

the regime in February 1982, the Ba'athists used the Defense Brigades[10] composed of people from the Alawite, Kurdish, and other minorities to suppress it. Nevertheless, after the revolt, while the Kurds were shown as partners in the regime of repression, the secular Alawite and Sunni Arabs were united against the Kurdish parties, and Assad became closer to the Sunni Arab sectors in 1985 (ibid., 62-67). There was often alliance between the Alawite and Sunni elites. They reinforced Syrian Arab nationalism, while the rights of Kurds were not regarded and they were at least partly Arabized and assimilated, especially as many of them did not have Syrian citizenship (See: Moaz, 1999, 67-68). In this regard, the Arabization of Kurdish areas increased the Islamization of Êzîdî Kurds (Yildiz, 2005, 24).

The Arab nationalists used religious development in the Syrian public arena and Islamification to silence Kurds, especially by intermingling Arabs and Kurds in various religious brotherhoods such as the Mystical orders. As the Iraqi Ba'ath regime used some of the Qadiriya sheikhs, between 1970 and 1990 the Syrian regime used the Kurdish Sufi sheikhs to influence the Kurdish community through their networks. For example, as already mentioned, Sheikh Ahmad Kuftaru, the popular spiritual leader of Kuftariyya branch of Naqshbandiyya and his order became a liaison between the regime and the Kurdish community. Another kind of religious brotherhood was promoted by Muhammad Sa'id Ramadan al-Bouti (1929-2013), a religious leader who supported the regime. Using Islamic discourse, and without denying his ethnic origins, al-Bouti, who was suspected of associating with the Muslim Brotherhood, encouraged the Kurdish–Arab brotherhood to advance in a peaceful and progressive manner towards the creation of an Islamic state. Nevertheless, al-Bouti was an advocate of the

---

[10] A paramilitary force founded in 1971 to defend the Assad government, which merged into the Syrian Arab Army as part of the Syrian Republican Guard forces in 1984.

regime and openly criticized the Muslim Brotherhood. Since representing the Kurdish community using the official discourse of Arabism was difficult, the regime as part of its political strategy utilzed these religious figures as official representatives of Islam and the Sunni majority of Kurds and Arabs in Syria to gain legitimacy and to silence both Sunni and Kurd opposition (Tejel, 2009, 65-6 & 95).

The Syrian regime supported such religious leaders while they were not against its politics. For example, Sheikh Muhammad Mashuk al-Khaznawi, a very popular Sufi, was backed by the regime because of his liberal and modernist reading of the Quran. But he was abandoned and seen as a potential threat to the regime when he supported the Kurdish movement during the "Qamishli revolt", followed by repression in 2004. His religious charisma, combined with nationalism, was popular with the Kurdish nationalist movement. Eventually his stance led to his assassination in 2005 followed by a demonstration of several thousand Kurds in Qamishli (ibid., 101-2 & 126).

In the early twenty-first century, as in the middle of twentieth century, the regime attributed Kurdish activities, even cultural ones, to Zionist propaganda. However, with the growth of Muslim Brotherhood activity, despite their leadership's declaration with regard to the cultural demands of the Kurds, the Kurdish forces feared the emergence of an Islamic power and an increase of the Sunni Arab majority in politics (ibid., 107 & 130). Following the Arab Spring in 2011, eventually disorder swept this country, too. The conflicts adopted a religious shape between pro-regime Alawites and anti-regime Sunnis (see: Ungor, 2020). This became clearer when each of them was supported by either Sunni or Shiite foreign states in the Middle East. The Kurds took part in the civil war. They followed a policy of mediation between the Alawite-Secular regime and Islamic opposition (Sunni-extremist forces), while the Ba'ath regime was seen as the preferred enemy. They used the above-mentioned situation in favour of their rights to make an autonomous administration.

IRAN: PERSIAN-KURDISH CONFRONTATION IN ROJHELAT

With the emergence of the Safavid Empire in the sixteenth century, Sunnism was gradually replaced and the Shiite sect became the state religion (see: Avery et al, 1991, 705; Jackson and Lockhart, 1986). The marriage between Shiism and politics gradually grew in favour of Fars/Persian ethnicity. Finally, it became a column of Fars-based Iranian nationalism which aimed to realize the Persians' dream of forming a homogenized unitary nation-state in the twentieth century. Today's Iran was a multi-ethnic confederation of different governments and dynasties until the second half of nineteenth century. There were principalities and local rulers in Rojhelat. Even during Iran's Constitutional Revolution (1905–1911), the first constitution considered a decentralized country including different states, provinces and districts with their assemblies and councils. But this was never implemented (see: Mofidi, 2019).

With the start of centralization in nineteenth century, the Kurdish revolts accelerated. After Sheikh Ubeydullah's uprising against both the Ottomans and Qajars in 1880, other revolts occurred at the end of the Qajar dynasty such as the revolt of Simko Shikak (1887–1930), a Kurdish nationalist leader, who declared an independent Kurdish state (1918-22) and aimed to extend it to the whole of Kurdistan (Romano, 2006, 222). In the Constitutional era and the early decades of twentieth century, religion was one of the important elements of communal identity in Kurdistan and Sunni clerics served as local retinues of tribal chieftains who were the active sector of the Kurdish population politically. The effect of this led to religious conflicts on the stance of political leaders (Vali, 2011, 7 & 11). Moreover, the Islamic propaganda of Turks during the First World War and their independence war affected the civil war in Kurdistan between the Muslim Shikak tribe and Christian Assyrians of whom it was suspected that the Allies, Russians and the British, backed (Fieldhouse, 2001, 81). These conflicts, as one of the factors, negatively affected the Simko's revolt which was eventually suppressed by Reza Khan, the Commander-in-Chief of the Qajar Army, who viewed different nationalities and ethnicities as the barrier to making the Pahlavi monarchy based on a unitary and Persian nation-state in 1925.

The Secular State of Pahlavi (1925-1979): a functional view of religion

The Iranian state based on the Mashruteh Constitution of 1906 was a Shiite state. Accordingly, Shia as the state religion was an element of Persian-Iranian nationalism during the Pahlavi period too (Avery et al, 1991, 426). Indeed, the Persian state emerged from the time of Reza Shah (1925–1941). It was a quasi-modern centralized state. Reza Shah used religion to gain power, publishing a fatwa (religious decree) from Shiite Ayatollahs Isfahani and Naini, declaring obedience to him a religious duty. Although as a Shiite Shah he took an oath to support the Shiite faith, his social policy was secular (ibid., 1991, 221-235 & 740). Nevertheless, relying on that religious support, Reza Shah as an anti-pluralist implemented a new centralization policy and introduced Persian nationalist strategies to Persianize society; he dismissed non-Persian identities as backward and instigated systematic attacks upon them. Due to the suffocating effect of his policies, there were no remarkable movements during his dictatorship (Akbarzadeh, 2019b). Persian was imposed on all

Iranians as the official language. So, throughout the 1920s and 1930s Reza Shah's reforms to liberate Kurdistan from tradition were perceived as a forced assimilation policy targeting the Kurds (Dehzani, 2008, 181). During the occupation of Iran during World War II, Reza Shah was exiled. His son, Mohammad Reza Shah, continued his father's policy.

After WWII, when the central government was weak, ethno-nationalist movements emerged. Although the discourse of the Kurdish Resurrection Society (JK)[1] founded on 16 August 1942, was primarily secular nationalism, it appealed to Islam mostly functionally and populistically because of the influence of Islam in Kurdish society (Vali, 2011, 20). In this regard, the Kurdish movement used the influence of the clergy in society. When JK transformed into the Kurdistan Democratic Party (KDP/KDPI), Qazi Muhammad, a famous religious figure and nationalist character was selected as its leader to constitute the Republic of Kurdistan in 1946. Although the political positions of nationalist intelligentsia and the discourse of the Republic were secular, because of the existence of a traditional society, a religious outlook and the general traditionalism of the intelligentsia, Quranic verses and prophetic tradition were incorporated into the discourse of Kurdistan. The religious notions and ethical precepts were invoked to legitimate authority and to serve populist political ends. There was a Union of Islamic Religious Scholars. As in other Muslim states, one of the most important ways to affect people was through religious tribunes. For example, the Kurdish government indoctrinated its progressive aims and political ideas into the mass through the Friday sermon. Mela Hussein Majdie, the Imam of Friday prayers in Mahabad regarded the government and Ghazi Muhammad's instructions on the purpose and content of the Friday sermon such that he emphasized the importance of ancient Kurdish

---

[1] Komeley Jiyanewey Kurd

civilization, national unity and the progress of the motherland (ibid., 106-7). Nevertheless, after 11 months of governing part of Kurdistan, the Kurdish government was attacked by the Iranian regime and collapsed. The regime, which strongly propagated Iranian nationalism, in 1946 used religion against the nationalistic movement in Kurdistan (Avery et al, 1991, 439). The Kurds were targeted as Sunni and also anti-religious people affiliated with the Communist Soviets. In order to execute by hanging the president of Kurdistan and his comrades, the regime forced some Kurdish Sunni clerics to sign the sentence, although other clerics refused. The execution documents of others also show that they were publicly executed after the Islamic ritual.[2] Thus, the regime portrayed the sentences as legitimate and the Kurdish nationalists as dissenters of both Iran and religion.

By continuing the Kurdish movement under the leadership of the KDP, the Shah's regime used religion against the Kurdish nationalists. The Kurds in Iran are religiously divided into Shiite and Sunni, though there are other small minorities. These religious cleavages have been used politically against Kurdish nationalism. During the Pahlavi regime, like its forerunners, the Shiite sect as a common religion between some sections of Kurds and Persian rulers paved the way for the implementation of the government's policies. The regime used this religion to keep the Shiite Kurds aloof from nationalist activities, as in the 1920s, 1946 and after 1979 (Bruinessen, 1992, 23). It even used social cleavages among Sunnis. For example, it constituted the 'party of Seyidan' in Mahabad during the early 1950s. The party's members were mostly Seyids[3], an influential religious stratum in traditional Islamic societies, and some low-ranking religious figures. The regime used them and motivated them to activate against the

---

[2] See: The report of Iranian Interior Ministry about executing four Kurdish officers in 7/4/1947, date: 14/4/1947, Iran National Archives, document n. 293-12/143/1.
[3] Seyid/Sayyid is an honorific title denoting people accepted as descendants of the prophet Muhammad through his daughter Fatimah and his cousin and son-in-law Ali.

activities of the KDP (Blouriyan, 1997, 118). The party of Seyidan was unable to succeed and was dissolved very soon afterwards.

Unlike the Shiite Kurdish priests, historically, the Sunni Kurdish priests (Mela/Mamostay Aiyni) had an important role in the revival of Kurdish identity socially, literarily and politically, as the only literate people and intellectual stratum in Kurdish traditional society before the development of modern education (Mofidi, 2017). Although they were generally conservative, some of them were active participants in the national liberation struggle, especially their key role in traditional Kurdish movements under the religious leaders. Nevertheless, the priests gradually became more conservative and were partly marginalized in the modern Kurdish movement under the leadership of political parties. This situation paved a way for the Iranian regime to implement its religious politics against the Kurds more successfully. Consequently, the Iranian authorities used this opportunity to attract Kurdish priests. As in other states overlapping Kurdistan, they "tried to reorganize the Sunni hierarchy by granting the Melas a monthly stipend, in the hope of bringing them round to serve the interests of the state" (Ghassemlou, 1993, 98). Thus, they succeeded to some extent and moved them partly away from the secular Kurdish nationalist movement. A policy which was continued more rigorously by the next regime.

The Islamic regime (1979-): religious discourse in the service of Persian nationalism

With the 1979 revolution and subsequently the establishment of the Islamic regime, "the emphasis on the Shiite nature of political power became more pronounced" (Tezcür and Asadzade, 2019). The ideological use of religion by religious leaders and politicians under the general leadership of Ayatollah

Khomeini during the 1979 revolution, led to religion contributing more to Perso-Iranian nationalism (Iraniyyat) discourse than in previous periods, which made Shiism and Persianism/Farsism (prioritizing the Fars ethnicity) the two main elements of this nationalism (Akbarzadeh, 2019b). Thus, the political function of religion became more manifest in the Islamic Republic of Iran (IRI). Shiite religious institutions were transferred to the centre of political power. The Twelver Shiite school of Islam was retained in the new constitution of 1979 as the official religion of Iran; the Supreme Leader of the regime could only be a high-ranking Shiite cleric; and the President of the country could only be a Shiite.[4]

Unlike the Fars-secular ethno-nationalism of the Shah's regime, moreover, the Fars-Shiite ethno-nationalism formed the basis of the Islamic regime's internal colonization strategies and domestic policies. The religious Perso-nationalist forces such as the Freedom Movement of Iran (FMI), Islamic Republic Party etc. increasingly reformulated 'Iranian identity' based on Shiism to homogenize society, which could serve 'the national integrity', given the fact that historically Sunni non-Persian regions have often been the epicentre of political resistance, especially in Kurdistan (Mohammadpour and Soleimani, 2020; Soleimani and Mohammadpour, 2019). In this regard, even the secular[5] Persian intellectuals paid attention to the importance of Shiism along with their Persianism. For example, Dariush Forouhar, leader of the Nation Party of Iran (NPI), defended Twelver Shiism as the official religion in the constitution.[6] Indeed, the Persian state and nationalists used the Shiite fundamentalism in Iran as another "technology of Othering" the non-Fars ethno-nations (Dehzani,

---

[4] See: The Constitution of the IRI, 1979, articles 12, 5, 107–9 and 115.
[5] The word 'secular', here, does not refer to anti-religion, but separation of 'state and religion', not 'religion and politics', as well as religious freedom.
[6] In this regard see the report of one of his speech published in: Kayhan newspaper, 14 October, 1979.

2008, 49).

Although the regime was based on Shiite fundamentalism and tried to extend Shiism, nevertheless, it laid claim to universalism as an Islamic regime for political aims. Islamic identity as a broader identity was used to facilitate uniting and mobilizing different social masses. The Islamic ideology and discourse helped the new regime to fight on various fronts. In the Islamic regime there had been no space for any competing nationalisms or ethnic political activities. The regime reinforced Islamic identity and promulgated Islamic brotherhood as the bond that holds together the diverse ethnicities and Islamic sects living in Iran. Talking with Sunnis and non-Persians, the Persian and Persianized leaders and politicians used the conception of Islamic Umma and brotherhood merely to cover ethno-religious distinctions. In his speech to a group of Kurdish people, Ayatollah Khomeini emphasized Islam as the instrument to forge unity and defuse separation between Kurds and Persians. He regularly warned Kurds against the idea of ethnic divisions (Akbarzadeh, 2019b). He had no tolerance towards what might threaten the Islamic state. Unlike Reza Shah, who saw ethno-national diversity as against modernity, Khomeini saw it as a threat to Islam and justified it under Muslim brotherhood, while for both of them ethnicity was a priority (Romano, 2006, 234). In the early years after the revolution, the secular leaders also used Islamic discourse against the various ethno-nationalist movements.[7] Thus, in an implicitly imperial-colonial orientation the regime did not recognize the self-determination rights of non-Persian ethno-nations, especially the Kurds who demanded them.

After the 1979 revolution, the Kurdish movement was powerful. The Kurdish parties controlled most of Rojhelat,

---

[7] For example, in his already mentioned speech, Forouhar highlighted the Kurds as "Iranian and Muslim" to cover their special identity and subsequently their special rights.

especially the Sunni areas, and demanded autonomy. The new regime first tried to buy time and strengthen itself. Then, as its second step, it used all means against the movement including suppression by force and violence. In line with the first step, it tried to reinforce an Islamic atmosphere in Kurdistan and negotiate with Kurdish groups. Despite its conflict with the Sunnism, the Shiite regime saw Kurdish nationalism as its greatest danger. Therefore, the regime first targeted secular groups which were more nationalistic and more oppositional, while having interaction with Sunni Islamic groups. The governmental politicians used the hegemony of Islamic discourse in the country and the influence of religion in Kurdish society against the secular Kurdish parties and organizations. They reinforced Islamic identity and extended their preferred Islamic ideology in Kurdistan in different ways, including propaganda through public media under the government's control, distributing Islamic publications, connecting with priests and so on. They also tried to create, recruit and manipulate different Sunni groups, especially those close to them. Thus, the regime exploited Islamic sentiments and Muslim brotherhood to influence the masses, as well as to move traditional ordinary people away from Kurdish nationalist parties.

Although the KDPI historically had a connection with the Sunni clergies, with the 1979 revolution some religious and religio-national groups emerged in Kurdistan like Maktab Quran (Qur'an School) and its Islamic Mosawat party, the Muslim Brotherhood trend, the Rizgari party[8] related to the Naqshbandi order, and the Khabat party, an ethno-national-religious group.

---

[8] The party, known as Sipay Rizgari (the Salvation Force), was a religious/Sufi party under Sheikh Madeh Sheikh Osman Sirajadin Naghshbandi. Due to some conflicts, especially the ideological dispute, Komele in Meriwan and Sine, and KDPI (around the time of its fourth congress) in Pawe and Hewramanat, disarmed Sipay Rizgari in 1980 (Author's interviews with various Kurdish personalities, notably Youssef Ardalan, one of the Komele ex-leaders in Sine after the 1979 revolution, 8/12/2021).

There were conflicts between secular and religious Kurds especially between the radical leftists/Komele and Islamists such as Maktab Qur'an and Rizgari. The regime used this religious-secular cleavage. For example, at the beginning it supported the Sunni Islamic movement including "Maktab Qur'an" and Muslim Brotherhood trends to aid their ideological conflicts with Marxists and secularists against the mainstream secular Kurdish movement under the leadership of KDPI and Komele[9], although it then suppressed them too (for details see: Mofidi, 2015b). Conversely, the Kurdish movement supported the opponents of the regime, especially the leftist groups.

On the other hand, the regime employed common religion and Shiite fundamentalism to silence the Shiite Kurds, to weaken Kurdish nationalism among them, and also to easily recruit them to fight against the Kurdish nationalist forces, mostly Sunni (see: Bruinessen, 2000). In fact, the regime used the religious conflicts between Sunni and Shiite Kurds to its advantage. It opened the door for the Shiites to access some higher levels of political power provided that they remained silent about their Kurdish identity. This use of religious politics was effective. Unlike in the Sunni Kurdish areas, Kurdish nationalists were less successful in mobilizing the Shiite Kurds. While large numbers of Kurds boycotted the Constitutional referendum, held in December 1979, and the participation of Sunni Kurds was very low in the first presidential elections in January 1980, a large majority of Shiite Kurds voted in favour of the constitution and participated in elections (see: Tezcür and Asadzade, 2019). Conversely, apart from Sunni Kurds, KDPI had some influence among Yarsan/Ahle-e-Hagh people, since the Islamic regime was against Yarsanism, an indigenous religion in Kurdistan.

Along with the above-mentioned activities, the regime also

---

[9] The Society of Revolutionary Toilers of Iranian Kurdistan, known as Komele/Komala, was a Marxist-Leninist Party founded in 1978. For more information about the party, see: Mofidi, 2016.

negotiated with different Kurdish groups. In reaction to the religious stance of the new regime in Tehran and its reliance on a set of religious tools for nationalistic aims, as well as for providing a common context and paving the way for negotiation, Abdul-Rahman Qasimlou (1930-1989), the ex-leader of the KDPI, and other Kurdish leaders were in some part forced to consider the political function of religion. After the 1979 revolution, in order to connect with religious figures, the KDPI reconstituted the Union of Islamic Religious Scholars, which related to the period of the Kurdistan Republic, under the Union of Religious Scholars (URS).[10] Moreover, secular Kurdish nationalists tried to use the influence of clerics and prominent religious figures including the city Friday Imams. Then, the Kurdish secular political parties intentionally selected a famous religious, but politically secular figure, Sheikh Ezzeddin Hussaini (1921-2011), as a common leader and head of the 'Council of Kurdish People' or the Kurdish People's Negotiation Mission, while Qasimlou was its spokesman, to negotiate with the regime's delegations (Koohi-Kamali, 1992, 182-3). In contrast to Khomeini, religious Kurdish leaders, especially Ezzeddin, emphasized the rights of all ethnicities and nations in Islam. They were against governance of Muslims by a single group. After a

---

[10] There is no written documentary, but based on oral history, the Union of Islamic Religious Scholars was established during the Republic of Kurdistan in 1946. It had some judges, one of whom was Mela Resul Khizri from Shino. After the 1979 revolution, Qasimlou revived it. Mamosta Ibdaghi and some others reconstituted the Union of Religious Scholars in Piranshar and surrounding areas, meeting in Sardasht and Mahabad. And some of them became armed too. They discussed receiving Zakat for Peshmarga (Pêşmerge). While some scholars believed the Zakat was possible, others believed it was not, because Zakat goes to Mojahed. The second group argued that the help of people should be as help/support for Peshmarga, not Zakat. For them, Peshmarga was defender/Modafee, not Mojahed. There are two different concepts; Siyal and Jihad. Siyal is for defending the land, honor and dignity (Sharaf and Karamat), but Jihad is just for war for God/La Elaha Ela Allah (there is no God except Allah). So they said Zakat was not possible but people should help the Peshmerga since it was Siyal. However, by the central government's reoccupying Kurdistan's cities, the activities of the Union were stopped. It was reconstituted under the Union of Iranian Kurdistan Religious Scholars (YZKAI) in 2007 inside Rojhelat secretly by some pro-KDPI clergies like Mela Ali Selaw and Mela Ismail, some of whom then moved to Southern Kurdistan (See: http://yzaki.blogspot.com/p/blog-page_9821.html).

three-month period of war between the central government and Kurdish forces, by way of restarting negotiations the Iranian authorities outlined the term "Islamic autonomy", and asked the Kurdish leaders to adopt such autonomy. They accepted and answered that their people are Muslim and they have no problem with that. Whilst apart from the stance of secular Kurds, Ahmad Muftizada (1933-1993), an influential religious figure and leader of Maktab Qur'an, had also demanded Islamic autonomy for Kurdistan in the context of political Islam. Nevertheless, the new regime did not even concede an Islamic autonomy for Kurdistan and in the end withdrew from it too. Thus, the peaceful ways and negotiations had no result and the Kurdish leaders openly declared that the state in reality acts against Islam (Cabi, 2020; Romano, 2006, 235).

At the second step, i.e. suppression, the regime resorted to religious decrees against the Kurdish movement and its leaders, accusing them of acting against the revolution. For instance, an elected Kurdish representative, Qasimlou, was not allowed to enter the Assembly of Experts of the Constitution (which functioned as Constituent Assembly) because of Ayatollah Khomeini's fatwa against him as a 'corrupter of the earth' (mofsid-e fil arz), a religious term similar to Moharebeh (enmity and waging war against God) used against dissidents, and the KDPI was banned. Khomeini denounced Qasimlou and Sheikh Ezzeddin as enemies of the Islamic Republic, and called the KDPI the 'party of Satan' (Akbarzadeh, 2019b; Koohi-Kamali, 1992, 184). Eventually, on 18-19 August 1979, Khomeini issued two decrees to the government's military forces authorizing fully-fledged repression of Kurdish forces (al-Khomeini, 2014, 61 & 278). Following Khomeini's Jihad order/fatwa against the Kurdish movement, the regime announced its war as a holy war between Islam and heresy (Kofr) and invaded Kurdish provinces by using both the religious and nationalist sentiments of the

Persian people to suppress the Kurdish national movement. The Islamic regime dispatched all its militia including regular military and the Islamic Revolutionary Guard Corps (IRGC henceforth), Hezbollahi (party of God) forces and Islamic Popular Mobility Units (IPMU, known as Basij) to Kurdistan (Koohi-Kamali, 1992, 184; Mohammadpour and Soleimani, 2020). They were accompanied by a death squad led by Sadeq Khalkhali, a clergyman and Khomeini's representative sent to accomplish the decrees in Kurdistan. On 20 August, he entered Kurdistan and immediately sentenced many Kurds to death and executed them (see; Cabi, 2020; Hassaniyan, 2019).

After three months of war in Kurdistan, by Khomeini's order it was stopped. Indeed, the cease-fire was temporary for the purpose of holding a referendum for the new constitution and the first elections, as well as to refresh the regime's forces. After few months, the regime resumed its invasion. It had achieved its goals and did not want to give concessions to the Kurdish forces. Moreover, it had attracted some Kurdish people in the name of Islam and created the military organization of 'Muslim Peshmargas,' affiliated to IRGC, versus the ordinary 'Kurdish Peshmargas', to fight the Kurdish nationalist parties (Koohi-Kamali, 1992, 188-9; Mofidi, 2017b). Even when Kurdish leaders were trying to solve the problem with a political approach, the commanders of IRGC announced that they would continue fighting against the 'unbelievers' even if a cease-fire were negotiated (Ward, 2009, 232-3). Finally, after a long and bitter war the liberated parts of Rojhelat were reoccupied.

During the war, to justify the regime's actions, the state-controlled media, the public Radio-TV, spread misinformation and labelled the Kurdish movement as an anti-religious and pro-Western force. For instance, they spread false stories alleging that "the Kurdish *Peshmerga* are kidnapping women and girls" and "the KDPI and Komele have shut down all mosques in

Kurdistan and people are not allowed to pray" (Hassaniyan, 2019). Moreover, based on Khomeini's fatwa against all non-religious (Kurdish and non-Kurdish) political parties and undesired communities, the executed Kurds (then even the Sunni leaders) were often buried in the extraordinary and unmarked cemeteries called La'nat Abad (the place of Accursed people) in Kurdish cities like Kirmashan, Wirmê/Urmiya, Bijar and Qurwe/Qorveh (Soleimani and Mohammadpour, 2019). Thus, the regime tried to present the Kurdish movement as anti-religion and to legitimize the executions as allowed by God. In fact, the majority of Kurds were Muslim and the parties respected the people's faith and accepted the Islamic autonomy. The regime indeed targeted Kurdish nationalism (Dehzani, 2008, 282). In the regime's discourse, the military occupation and securitizing of Rojhelat were considered as the conquest of (Fath-e) Kurdistan, thus indicating the conquest of Muslims over non-Muslim lands (Soleimani and Mohammadpour, 2019).

With the reoccupation of Kurdistan's cities by the central government, the activities of the URS were stopped. Afterwards, in 1981 the regime established an institution under "Markaze Bozorge Islami" (The Great Islamic Center) with branches in major Kurdish cities to supervise and manipulate the religious rituals, events and endowments of Sunni communities, to organize Sunni religious students, and to restrict religious dissidents and independent Melas in collaboration with intelligence services. Those Melas who refused to collaborate were accused of being anti-Revolutionary, Maktabi, Wahhabi and Zionist (Mohammadpour and Soleimani, 2020). Thus, much more than the Pahlavi regime, the Islamic regime used the governmental Sunni priests against the Kurdish movement. They were even used to encourage ordinary Kurds to conscript into the regime's armies. For example, a Kurdish conscript in the 1980s war, narrated his memory of that time as such: "In his speech before our attack, the Friday Imam of Sine told us that when we are pursuing the KDPI and Komele, God rewards us as much as the turning of our vehicles' wheels."[11]

In following decades, the regime continued to use religious rituals and ceremonies among Sunni Kurds, to control them through their affiliated priests and clergies. As well, it started to reshape the historico-religious space of Kurdistan through relocating and dispersing Shiites, often non-Kurds, among the Sunni-Kurdish population to suppress them. It established a number of Shiite centres in Sunni regions of Rojhelat, while prohibiting Sunni centres in the predominantly Shiite regions (see: Mohammadpour and Soleimani, 2020). Conversely, not only moderate Sunni groups like Maktab Quran and Muslim Brotherhood trends continued their activities, but also radical Sunni groups like Salafists emerged, although some of these new religious groups were used by the regime against the secular Kurdish parties. Moreover, along with the political and military activities of Kurdish nationalist forces, in order to oppose and neutralize the regime's religious politics, the KDPI reconstituted URS under the Union of Iranian Kurdistan Religious Scholars (UIKRS/YZAKI) in 2007, based in Başûr, with secret members inside Rojhelat. In contrast, the regime continued to respond harshly to the Kurdish nationalist political activists, as well as radical Sunnis, especially Jihadi Salafists, by killing and executing them under religious slogans (Akbarzadeh, 2019b). For example, 'between 2007 and 2016, at least 22 of the activists were executed, on the charges of committing Moharebeh' (Tezcür and Asadzade, 2019).

In short, both parties tried to do what they could. The regime eventually did not accept any demands from the Kurds, while the Kurds resisted. After suppressing the Kurdish secular

---

[11] In the author's interview with him.

movement, the regime suppressed the Sunni-Kurdish Islamic groups too. The Perso-Iranian nationalists, religious and non-religious, were all against the Kurdish movement. Nevertheless, the war and conflict between Kurdish and Persian nationalists is still continuing.

CONCLUSION

As ancient empires, Sassanids and Romans, then Islamic empires, Ottomans and Safavids, the contemporary states and nationalists in the Middle East have politically used religion especially in state and nation construction, nationalism and nationalistic confrontations. Since the societies in the region are still traditional and religion has more influence there, in the nationalistic confrontations, religion has had a political function for religious and non-religious nationalists. In the four countries overlapping Kurdistan, religion whether as part of a nationalism or a nationalist system, or a legitimizing and mobilizing means, has had political function. The governments and political groups of dominant ethno-nations, i.e. Turks, Persians and Arabs, have used it for nation-construction and assimilation of others. In this regard, as Bahcheli & Noel (2010) mention about Turkey, in Iran, Iraq and Syria also the religious parties have no less nationalistic stands than the secular parties in relation to the Kurdish issue. Indeed, according to Zubaida (1992, 8), Islamists in practice have not followed the claim of the anti-nationalist logic of pan-Islamism. Thus, during the twentieth century (and so far in unliberated parts of Kurdistan) the Kurds were victims more innocent than the Jews in the first half of the century, described by Hannah Arendt (1958, 5-6) using the scapegoat theory. The dominant sinful people sacrifice Kurds to remove their sins.

In relation to the above-mentioned situation of the Kurds and Kurdistan, the role of Western powers should not be ignored. Although the issue of the right of nations to self-determination has been raised by both Eastern and Western political leaders since the second decade of the twentieth century, a policy with a nineteenth century territorialized understanding of nationhood was implemented in the Middle East. On the one hand, they imposed some unitary states on diverse peoples and tried to create a homogenous identity in each created country, while they themselves followed a sectarian view to govern these countries. On the other hand, politics based on their economic interests in the region led to the creation of many states for the Arabs, some of them having a population of only a few thousand, while ignoring millions of Kurds. Indeed, at the time there were still tribal societies within different ethnic groups of Arabs, Turks, Persians and Kurds, with no modern understanding of nation among them. An ethnicity and its territory could be a basis for a nation, and consequently the creation of a nation-state, instead of the imposition of some states whose territories do not conform to human borders or ethnic territories. However, they did not consider the compatibility of political and social structures. Such politics affected the socio-political situation in the region and Kurdistan, so that afterwards the dominant ethno-nations in the new independent states not only continued the religious politics inherited from previous empires but also followed the Western powers' sectarian politics and their territorialized understanding of nationhood. This led to flouting the rights of the large ethno-national community of Kurds, subsequent conflicts and a lack of peace in the region for long time.

Unlike the perception of nationhood which was indeed an imperfect understanding of nation-state by politicians, during the twentieth century the political rights of ethno-nations gradually found more importance, leading to a different awareness of nationhood and consideration of the ethno-national diversity in politics. Consequently, various political systems changed and even some new nation-states emerged. Indeed, an ethno-nationalized understanding of nation-state materialized in which social structures and characteristics of people/nation became more of a determinant than a state territory, some parts of which were seen as colonies or occupied the lands of dominated ethno-nations. In other words, for them the concepts of *nation* and *state* were not rigidly tied and intertwined.

Despite such changes, the imperfect understanding of nationhood continued in the Middle East, whereas if there had been a correct understanding of the theory of nation-state from the beginning, so that each large ethno-nation had at least a state with respect for the rights of smaller minorities at various political levels, the politics in the region might be different and more peaceful. However, the legacy of Western powers was the creation of some undemocratic states that, under the chauvinist views of dominant ethno-nations, led to internal colonization and long-running conflicts in the Middle East, especially in Kurdistan. The existence of a traditional society and religious intellectual heritage among Kurds also contributed to this process. In the conflicts, the opposing parties used any means against each other and justified it with religion. Thus, religion as one of the important social factors in the region, instead of strengthening equality and peace, became a tool in the hands of the dominant ethno-nations for the purpose of colonization, exploitation and assimilation. In contrast, the dominated ethno-nations also resorted to the same means to resist and thwart such politics. These confrontations increased the political function of religion.

Studying different nationalisms in the region shows the political importance of religion for nationalists and politicians. Seeing Islam as a column of Arabic nationalism and emphasizing it as a religion special to Arab people, although it was also a universal religion, the Arab nationalists such as Abd al-Rahman al-Bazzaz, Zurayq, Aflagh and so on, some of whom were Christian (see: Kedourie, 1992, 326-327), tried to use it exclusively and to deprive other rival nationalisms of Sunni Islam. This was true of the Kurdish nationalism in Iraq and Syria, and practically turned it against Islam so that any enmity with Arab nationalism was considered as enmity with Islam. Same as the Arab nationalists, Persian nationalists in Iran tried to use the Shiite sect as a special sect for them. After the 1979 revolution, the Islamic regime also reinforced Perso-Iranian nationalism to the detriment of Kurdish and other nationalisms, and religion was openly used against them.

Compared with the Arab and Persian nationalisms, the Turkish and Kurdish nationalisms were fundamentally more secular, although their relevant nationalists also considered the political function of religion. Indeed, although not one of the bases or part of their nationalisms, religion nevertheless was an important social factor in their societies: It occupied part of their politics, especially in nationalistic confrontations for legitimating their acts and demands, as well as mobilizing masses, creating solidarity and encouraging their forces. For example, the Turkish nationalists used religious discourse and conflicts for legitimizing their nationalist activities and mobilizing people in Turkey and Kurdistan in favour of their politics. Although the Turkish state claimed secularism, it was created based on the caliphate legacy and Islamic claims against non-Muslim foreign forces at the beginning of the construction of the Turkish state. In this regard, the secular Turkish nationalists used the so-called Muslim brotherhood to silence Kurdish nationalism, while at the same time under secularism, attracted the Alevis. Afterwards, the Islamist nationalists in Turkey also used a communalist conflict between Sunni and Alevi Kurds in the 1970s, reinforcing Sunnism by deploying right-wing forces. Thus, Turkish Islamism was in favour of Turkish ethno-nationalism (Zubaida, 1992, 8).

In each of the four countries, the majority of parties involved were Muslim, whether Kurds or non-Kurds, while the state ethno-nationalists justified their own nationalist measures by religion and portrayed Kurdish nationalism as anti-religion. Often, they even expressed their repressive actions, using religious notions such as 'holy war' and 'conquest', to justify the suppression of Kurdish forces as non-Muslim whose land had to be occupied.

The states' dominant ethno-nationalists used religious sentiments and Islamic discourse to cover the ethno-national divisions between dominant and dominated ethno-nations. Islam as an umbrella was often used for national solidarity and unity. In this vein, in the Middle Eastern states, minorities were generally defined in terms of their religious distinctiveness from the Muslim majority. So, in their constitutions such as those of Turkey and Iran, the Kurds were not recognized as a minority. Since the majority of Kurds in the four countries were Muslim, Islam was used to prevent the Kurds from being recognized as distinct from the ethno-national majorities of Turks, Fars and Arabs in each country (Gourlay, 2020). On the other hand, along with their use of Islam to consolidate themselves, the states tried to reinforce the religious cleavages and minorities in Kurdistan to prevent solidarity in Kurdish society. They divided and ruled. For a long time, thus, the Kurdish movement and politics in Greater Kurdistan were afflicted by religious cleavages in favour of the states. The effect was such that, according to Bozarsalan (2003b), the Kurdish movement was not able 'to integrate the religious communities, Sunni, Shiite, Alevi, Yarsan, Êzîdî or establish unitary strategies across state borders' (p. 38).[1]

Against dominant ethno-nations, the Kurdish nationalist

---

[1] According to Türkmen (2018), "about 15% of the Kurdish population in Turkey is estimated to be Alevis." About Alevis and diversity of religions in Kurdistan also see: Bruinessen, 1996; Bruinessen, 2000; White, 2000, 41-42, Keles, 2014.

movement also became intertwined with religion at the beginning of its emergence. The religious figures who entered the movement, like Sheikh Said, Sheikh Mahmoud etc. used a religious language in their nationalist struggle. In fact, they helped to propagate and accept the nationalist concepts in Kurdistan. Nevertheless, because of the lack of a Kurdish state and government, religion had little political function for Kurdish nationalism, and the Kurdish nationalists were unable to use it appropriately. Meanwhile, accessing various resources through state and governmental organizations, the dominant ethno-nationalists used the influence of religion in society, religious institutes and groups against Kurdish nationalism. All having their own ethno-national rights while tying their religious and ethnic identities to each other, they reinforced Islamic identity against Kurdish identity among the Kurds. They centralized the religious establishments to control and organize the religious rituals and events, to attract the Kurdish clerics and religious people and to separate them from Kurdish nationalists by religious propaganda. However, the Kurdish movement resisted. Thus, the confrontations between different nationalists, namely Kurdish-others (Persian, Turkish and Arab), continued in the four countries.

BIBLIOGRAPHY

Akbarzadeh, S., Ahmed Z. S., Laoutides C. & Gourlay W. (2019b): "The Kurds in Iran: balancing national and ethnic identity in a securitized environment", *Third World Quarterly*, DOI: 10.1080/01436597.2019.1592671

Akbarzadeh, S., Laoutides C., Gourlay W. & Ahmed Z. S. (2019a). "The Iranian Kurds' Transnational Links: Impacts on Mobilization and Political Ambitions," *Ethnic and Racial Studies*, DOI: 10.1080/01419870.2019.1689280

Al-Khomeini, R. (2014), *Sahifeh-ye Imam*, its English translation, 22 volumes, V. 9, The Institute for Compilation and Publication of Imam Khomeini's Works.

Apter D. E. (1963), "Political Religion in the New Nations." In *Old Societies and New States; The quest for modernity in Asia and Africa*, edited by Clifford Geertz, London; Macmillan, pp. 57-104.

Arendt, H. (1958). *The Origins of Totalitarianism*, USA: Meridian Book.

Aronoff, M. J. (1974), *Frontiertown; The Politics of Community Building in Israel*, Manchester University Press.

Asad, T., "Religion, Nation-State, Secularism," in *Nation and Religion; Perspectives on Europe and Asia*, edited by Peter Van der Veer and Hartmut Lehmann, Princeton University Press, 1999, pp. 178-196.

Avery, P., Hambly G. and Melville C. (ed.)(1991), *From Nadir Shah to the Islamic Republic*, The Cambridge History Of Iran, in seven volume, volume 7, UK; Cambridge University Press.

Aziz, S. and Kirmanj S. (2018), "Iran's regional hegemony and Kurdish independence". In Alex Danilovich (ed.), *Federalism, Secession, and International Recognition Regime; Iraqi Kurdistan*, New York; Routledge, pp. 147-163.

Bahcheli, T. and Noel S. (2010), "The Justice and Development Party and the Kurdish Question," in *Nationalisms and Politics in Turkey; Political Islam, Kemalism and the Kurdish Issue*, eds. Marlies Casier and Joost Jongerden, Routledge.

Balibar, E. (1994), Masses, Classes, Ideas, Studies on politics and philosophy before and after Marx, translated by James Swenson, New York;

Routletdge.

Barker P. W. (2009), *Religious Nationalism in Modern Europe; if God be for us*, Routledge.

Barkey, H. J. and Fuller G. E. (1998), *Turkey's Kurdish Question*, USA; Rowman & Littlefield.

Bluriyan, G. (1997). *Alacoc; My Political Memories, Stockholm*, Forfattares Bokmaskin.

Borg, M. Ter B. and Henten J. W. V. (2010), *Powers; Religion as a Social and Spiritual Force*, New York; Fordham university press.

Bozarsalan, H. (1992), "The Political Aspects of the Kurdish Problem in Contemporary Turkey". In *The Kurds; A Contemporary Overview*, Philip G. Kreyenbroek and Stefan Sperl (eds.), London; Routledge, pp. 95-114.

Bozarsalan, H. (2003a), "Alevism and the Myths of Research: The Need for a New Research Agenda," in Paul J. White and Joost Jongerden (eds.), *Turkey's Alevi Enigma; A Comprehensive Overview*, Leiden; Brill, pp. 3-16.

Bozarsalan, H. (2003b), "Some Remarks on Kurdish Historiographical Discourse in Turkey (1919-1980)". In *Essays on the Origins of Kurdish nationalism*, Edited by: Abbas Vali, Mazda Publisher, 2003, pp. 14-39.

Bozarsalan, H. (2003c), "Kurdish Nationalism in Turkey: From Tacit Contract to Rebellion (1919-1925)". In *Essays on the Origins of Kurdish nationalism*, Edited by: Abbas Vali, Mazda Publisher, 2003, pp. 163-190.

Breuilly, J. (1993), *Nationalism and the State*, Manchester University press.

Bruinessen, M. V. (1992), *Agha, Shaikh and State, The Social and Political structures of Kurdistan*, London and New Jersey: Zed Books.

Bruinessen, M. V. (1996), "Kurds, Turks and the Alevi revival in Turkey," *Middle East Reports*, no. 200, pp 7-10.

Bruinessen, M. V. (1999), "The Kurds and Islam," *Islamic Area Studies project*, no. 13, Tokyo.

Bruinessen, M. V. (2000), *Mullas, Sufis and Heretics: The Role of Religion in Kurdish Society*. Collected articles. Istanbul: The Isis Press.

Cabi, M. (2020), "The roots and the consequences of the 1979 Iranian revolution: A Kurdish perspective," *Middle Eastern Studies*: https://doi.org/10.1080/00263206.2020.1722651

Chelik, A. B. (2003), "Alevis, Kurds and Hemshahris: Alevi Kurdish Revival in the Ninties," in Paul J. White and Joost Jongerden (eds.), *Turkey's Alevi Enigma; A Comprehensive Overview*, Leiden; Brill, pp. 141-157.

David E. A. (1963), "Political Religion in the New Nations." In *Old Societies and New States; The quest for modernity in Asia and Africa*, edited by Clifford Geertz, London; Macmillan, pp. 57-104.

Dehzani, J. (2008), "Nihilism and Technologies of Othering: The Kurds in

Iran, Iraq and Turkey," PhD diss., Carleton University, Canada.

Deniz, D. (2020) "Re-assessing the Genocide of Kurdish Alevis in Dersim, 1937-38," *Genocide Studies and Prevention*: An International Journal: Vol. 14: Iss. 2: 20-43. DOI: https://doi.org/10.5038/1911-9933.14.2.1728

Elitsoy, Z. A. (2017), "The Kurdish Hizbullah and Its Shifting Attitude towards Kurdishness and the Kurdish Issue in Turkey," *Fritillaria kurdica. Bulletin of Kurdish Studies* | NO. 17, pp.4-19.

Farrokh, K. (2011). *Iran at War 1500-1988*, UK; Osprey publishing.

Fieldhouse, D. K. (2001), *Kurds, Arabs and Britons; The Memoir of Lieutenant-Colonel W. A. Lyon CBE in Iraq 1918–44*, London; I.B.Tauris & Co Ltd.

Friedland, R. (2001). "Religious Nationalism and the Problem of Collective Representation." *Annual Review Sociology*, 27: 125-152. Accessed at: www.annualreviews.org.

Friedland, R. (2012), "The constitution of Religious Political Violence: Institution, Culture, and Power," in, *The Oxford Handbook of Cultural Sociology*, edited by Jeffery C. Alexander, Ronald N. Jacobs and Philip Smith, Oxford university press, 2012, pp. 429-470.

Fuccaro, N. (2003). "Kurds and Kurdish Nationalism in Mandatory Syria: Politics, Culture and Identity". In *Essays on the Origins of Kurdish nationalism*, Edited by: Abbas Vali, Mazda Publisher, 2003, pp. 191-217.

Ghassemlou, A. R. (1993), "Kurdistan in Iran." In Gerard Chaliand (ed.), *A People without a country, The Kurds and Kurdistan*, London: Zed Books, 1993, pp. 95-121.

Gorski, P. and Gulay T. (2013), "Religion, Nationalism, and Violence: An Integrated Approach," The *Annual Review of Sociology*, 39:193–210, doi: 10.1146/annurev-soc-071312-145641

Gottlieb, G. A. G. (1994), "Nations without States," *Foreign Affairs, Volume 73, No.3*, pp 100-112.

Gourlay, W. (2020) Beyond 'brotherhood' and the 'caliphate': Kurdish relationships to Islam in an era of AKP authoritarianism and ISIS terror, *British Journal of Middle Eastern Studies*, 47:4, 612-631, DOI: 10.1080/13530194.2018.1534679

Guibernau, M. (1999), *Nations without States; Political Communities in a Global Age*, UK; Polity Press.

Gunes, C. (2012), *The Kurdish National Movement in Turkey; From Protest to Resistance*, New York; Routledge.

Gunter, M. M. (2011), *The Kurds Ascending; the Evolving Solution to the Kurdish Problem in Iraq and Turkey, second edition*, New York; Palgrave Macmilan.

Gunter, M. M. (2018), *Historical Dictionary of the Kurds*, Third Edition, Rowman & Littlefield.

Hassaniyan, A. (2019), "Non-Violent Resistance in Iranian Kurdistan After 1979," *Journal of Ethnic and Cultural Studies*, Vol. 6, No. 3, 98-110. http://dx.doi.org/10.29333/ejecs/266

Hassanpour, A. (2003), "The Making of Kurdish Identity: Pre-20th Century Historical and Literary Discourses." In Abbas Vali (Ed.), *Essays on the Origins of Kurdish nationalism*, Mazda Publisher, pp. 106-162.

Hastings, A. (1999), *The Construction of Nationhood; Ethnicity, Religion and Nationalism*, Cambridge University Press.

Jackson, P. and Lockhart L. (eds.) (1986), *The Timurid and Safavid Periods*, The Cambridge History of Iran, in seven volume, volume 6, CAMBRIDGE UNIVERSITY PRESS.

Jongerden, J. (2003), "Violation of Human Rights and the Alevis in Turkey" in Paul J. White and Joost Jongerden (eds.), *Turkey's Alevi Enigma; A Comprehensive Overview*, Leiden; Brill, pp. 71-89.

Juergensmeyer, M. (2010). "Symbolic Violence; Religion and Empowerment", in *Powers; Religion as a Social and Spiritual Force,* Meerten B. Ter Borg and Jan Willem Van Henten, New York; Fordham university press, pp. 39-50.

Karadaghi, K. (1993). "The two Gulf wars: The Kurds on the World stage, 1979-1992," in *A People without a Country, The Kurds and Kurdistan*, Edited by Gerard Chaliand, London: Zed Books, 2014-230.

Kedourie, E. (1992), *Politics in the Middle East*, New York; Oxford University Press.

Kehl-Bodrogi, K. (2003), "Ataturk and the Alevis: A Holy Alliance?" in Paul J. White and Joost Jongerden (eds.), *Turkey's Alevi Enigma; A Comprehensive Overview*, Leiden; Brill, pp. 53-69.

Keles, J. Y. (2014), "The Politics of Religious and Ethnic Identity among Kurdish Alevis in the Homeland and in Diaspora," in Omarkhali, Khanna (ed.), *Religious Minorities in Kurdistan: Beyond the Mainstream.* Series: Studies in Oriental Religions, vol. 68. Harr, Publisher: Studies in Oriental Religions, vol. 68. Harrassowitz, Wiesbaden, 2014, pp.173–224.

Khoury, P. S. (1987), Syria and the French Mandate: The Politics of Arab Nationalism, 1920-1945. London: I.B. Tauris.

Kirmanj, S. and Rafaat A. (2020), "The Kurdish genocide in Iraq: the Security-Anfal and the Identity-Anfal," *journal of National Identities*, https://doi.org/10.1080/14608944.2020.1746250

Koohi-Kamali, F. (1992), "The development of nationalism in Iranian Kurdistan". In *The Kurds; A Contemporary Overview*, Philip G. Kreyenbroek and Stefan Sperl (eds.), London; Routledge, pp. 171-192.

Leezenberg, M. (2003), "Kurdish Alevis and the Kurdish Nationalist

Movement in the 1990s," in Paul J. White and Joost Jongerden (eds.), *Turkey's Alevi Enigma; A Comprehensive Overview*, Leiden; Brill, pp. 197-212.

Maóz, M. (1999), *Middle eastern Minorities between integration and conflict*, The Washington Institute for Near East Policy.

Marcus, A. (1993), "Turkey's Kurds after the Gulf War: a Report from the Southeast," in *A People without a country; The Kurds and Kurdistan*, Edited by Gerard Chaliand, London: Zed Books, pp. 238-247.

Marx, K. and Engels, F. (1967), *The Communist Manifesto*, England; Penguin Books.

McDowall, D. (1992). "The Kurdish Question: A Historical Review". In *The Kurds; A Contemporary Overview*, Philip G. Kreyenbroek and Stefan Sperl (eds.), London; Routledge, pp. 10-32.

Mofidi, S. (2015a). *The Political function of religion in contemporary India (Hinduism and Islam)*, New Delhi: Swastik Publications.

Mofidi, S. (2015b). "Religion and Politics in Eastern Kurdistan (With a Focus on Maktab Qur'an During Iranian Revolution, 1979)", *Journal of Politics and Law*, Vol. 8, No. 3, pp. 36-50.

Mofidi, S. (2015c), "The Process of Leading Change in the Kurdistan Islamic Movement – Iraq (Emergence, Factors and Trends)." *Bulletin of Kurdish Studies*, No 7-8/03, Section of Kurdish Studies, Jagiellonian University, Kraków, Poland. Pp. 15-37.

Mofidi, S. (2016), The Left Movement and National Question; From Romanticism to Realism (With a Focus on Komala Organization), *Journal of Ethnic and Cultural Studies*, Vol. 3, No. 1, pp. 20-48.

Mofidi, S. (2017). "The Role of Clergy and Theologues in Creating a Kurdistani Relationship and the Spirit of Kurdish Nationalism" (in Kurdish), *KCCRC*, 16/07/2017, at: http://www.kurdistanc.com/Islamic/details.aspx?jimare= 5166

Mofidi, S. (2019). "Social Contract and Democratic Validity of Constitution (With a Focus on Iran and Iraq)," *International Journal of Human Rights and Constitutional Studies*, Vol. 6, No. 3, pp. 239-248. DOI: 10.1504/IJHRCS.2019.10019224

Mofidi, S. (2021a) "Kurdistan under the Impact of Religio-Political Confrontations of Ancient Empires (From the Median Empire to the Advent of Islam)," *Review of History and Political Science*, Vol. 9 No. 2.

Mofidi, S. (2021b), "Studying the Impact of Religio-Political Confrontations of Islamic Empires in Kurdistan (From the Beginning until the End of the Islamic Caliphate)," *Indonesian Journal of Islamic History and Culture*, Vol. 2 No. 1, pp. 1-49, https://doi.org/10.22373/ijihc.v2i1.830

Mofidi, S. and Rahmani S. (2018). "ISIS and Modernity; Studying the Effect of Middle-eastern quasi-modern States", *Research Letter of Political Science, Journal of Iranian Political Sciences Association*, V. 13, N. 2, pp. 157-186.

Mohammadpour, A. & Soleimani K. (2020). "'Minoritisation' of the other: the Iranian theo-ethnocratic state's assimilatory strategies," *Postcolonial Studies*, https://doi.org/10.1080/13688790.2020.1746157

Murphey, R. (1999). *Ottoman Warfare 1500-1700*, UK; UCL Press.

Nazdar, M. (1993). "The Kurds in Syria", in *A People without a country; The Kurds and Kurdistan*, Edited by Gerard Chaliand, London: Zed Books, Pp. 194-201.

Nottingham, E. K. (1971), *Religion; a sociological View*, New York: Random House INC.

Ocalan, A. (2002). *From Sumerian Clerical State towards Democratic Civilization*, ARD Publication centre, 2 volumes (in Persian).

Ocalan, A. (2006*). History in the basin of Tigris and Euphrates; Urfa the symbol of holiness and curse, Urfa defences*, Publication of works and thoughts of Abdullah Ocalan (in Persian).

Ocalan, A. (2018). *Manifesto for a Democratic Civilization*, Publication of works and thoughts of Abdullah Ocalan, 5 volumes, third edition (in Persian).

Olson, R. (1989), *The Emergence of Kurdish Nationalism and the Sheikh Said Rebellion, 1880–1925*, the University of Texas Press.

Omer, A. and Springs J. A. (2013). *Religious Nationalism; A Reference Handbook*, contemporary world issues series (ABC - CLID).

Orhan, M. (2016), Political Violence and Kurds in Turkey: Fragmentations, Mobilizations, Participation and Repertoires, Routledge.

Pentassuglia, G. (2020), "Assessing the Consistency of Kurdish Democratic Autonomy with International Human Rights Law," *Nordic journal of international law*, pp. 1-41. doi:10.1163/15718107-bja10013

Rafaat, A. (2018), Kurdistan in Iraq; The evolution of a quasi-state, New York; Routledge.

Raines, J. (2002). *Marx on Religion*. Philadelphia: Temple University Press.

Romano, D. (2006), *The Kurdish Nationalist Movement; Opportunity, Mobilization and Identity*, Cambridge University Press.

Schøtt, A. S. (2017). "The Kurds of Syria; From the Forgotten People to World-Stage Actors," Royal Danish Defence College, Copenhagen.

Soleimani, K. & Mohammadpour A. (2019). "The securitization of life: Eastern Kurdistan under the rule of a Perso-Shi'i state," *Third World Quarterly*, DOI: 10.1080/01436597.2019.1695199

Soleimani, K. (2018), "A Kurdish Sufi Master and His Christian Neighbors." Zanj: *The Journal of Critical Global South Studies*, vol. 2, no. 1, pp. 6–21.

Spinoza, B. (or Baruch) (2017). *Treatise on Theology and Politics (*A Theological-

Political Treatise), available at: https://www.earlymoderntexts.com/
assets/pdfs/spinoza1669.pdf.

Stoddard, T. L. (1917), "Pan-Turanism," *The American Political Science Review*,
Vol. 11, No. 1, pp. 12-23.

Tejel, J. (2009), *Syria's Kurds; History, politics and society*, Translated from the
French by Emily Welle and Jane Welle, Routledge.

Tezcür, G. M. and Asadzade P. (2019), "Ethnic nationalism versus religious
loyalty: The case of Kurds in Iran," *Nations and Nationalism* 25 (2), 652–
672. DOI: 10.1111/nana.12424

Türkmen, G. (2018), "Negotiating Symbolic Boundaries in Conflict
Resolution: Religion and Ethnicity in Turkey's Kurdish Conflict,"
Qualitative Sociology 41:569–591, https://doi.org/10.1007/s11133-018-
9400-4

Ungor, U. U. (2020). "Shabbiha: Paramilitary groups, mass violence and
social polarization in Homs," *Violence: An international journal*, Sage, pp. 1-
21, DOI: 10.1177/2633002420907771

Vali, A. (2003), "Genealogies of the Kurds: Constructions of Nation and
National Identity in Kurdish Historical Writing." In Abbas Vali (Ed.),
Essays on the Origins of Kurdish nationalism, Mazda Publisher, pp. 58-105.

Vali, A. (2011). *Kurds and the State in Iran; The Making of Kurdish Identity*,
London: I.B.Tauris & Co Ltd.

Van der Veer, P. (2010). "The Visible and the Invisible in South Asia". In
Powers; Religion as a Social and Spiritual Force, edited by Meerten B. Ter Borg
and Jan Willem Van Henten, New York; Fordham University press, pp.
103-115.

Van der Veer, P. and Lehmann H. (1999) (eds.), *Nation and Religion;
Perspectives on Europe and Asia*, Princeton University Press.

Vanly, I. c. (1968), The Kurdish Problem in Syria; Plans for the Genocide of
a National Minority, published by the Committee for the Defence of the
Kurdish People's Rights.

Vanly, I. C. (1992), "The Kurds in Syria and Lebanon". In *The Kurds; A
Contemporary Overview*, Philip G. Kreyenbroek and Stefan Sperl (eds.),
London; Routledge, pp. 143-170.

Vorhoff, K. (2003), "The Past in the Future: Discourses on the Alevis in
Contemporary Turkey," in Paul J. White and Joost Jongerden (eds.),
Turkey's Alevi Enigma; A Comprehensive Overview, Leiden; Brill, pp. 93-109.

Ward, S. R.(2009), *Immortal; A Military History of Iran and Its Armed Forces*,
Washington D.C; Georgetown University Press.

Weber, M. (1965). *The Sociology of Religion*, London: Tr. E. fischoff, Methuen
& Co Ltd.

White, P. J. (2000), *Primitive Rebels or Revolutionary Modernizers? The Kurdish National Movement in Turkey*, Zed Books.

Xenophon (1949). *The Persian Expedition*, translated by Rex Warner, The Penguin Books, First published.

Yavuz, M. H. (2007), "Five Stages of the Construction of Kurdish Nationalism in Turkey", in Charles G. MacDonald and Carole A. O'Leary, *Kurdish Identity; Human Rights and Political Status*, University Press of Florida, pp 56-76.

Yavuz, M. H. and Özcan N. A. (2006), "The Kurdish Question and Turkey's Justice and Development Party," *Middle East Policy*, Vol. Xiii, No. 1, pp. 102-119.

Yildiz, K. (2005), *The Kurds in Syria; The Forgotten People*, first published, London; Pluto Press.

Zubaida, S. (1992), "Introduction". In *The Kurds; A Contemporary Overview*, Philip G. Kreyenbroek and Stefan Sperl (eds.), London; Routledge, pp. 1-9.

www.ingramcontent.com/pod-product-compliance
Lightning Source LLC
Chambersburg PA
CBHW050655270326
41927CB00012B/3044